THE ORIGIN AND DEVELOPMENT OF THE SAROD

A Classical Musical Instrument

Avijit Ghosh

KALPAZ

The Origin and Development of the Sarod

ISBN : 978-81-7835-908-3

Published in 2012 in India by
Kalpaz Publications
C-30, Satyawati Nagar,
Delhi - 110052
E-mail: kalpaz@hotmail.com
Ph.: 9212729499

Lasser Type Setting : Rajender Vashist, Delhi
Printed at : Chawla Offset Printers, Delhi

Dedicated to the
Lotus feet's of
My Parents...

CONTENTS

LIST OF FIGURES AND PHOTOGRAPHS

FOREWORD

When I started taking my lessons in History, in early 1980's, nothing was to be read except the themes found from facts and evidence of the official state archives. There were several 'silences' in History of which I could not find any proper answer. There was nothing except virtual thinking; no questioning about the many dark corners of the past. I passed my examinations after an exact policing over my linguistic expertise on the established facts, while my thirst for knowing the past in a holistic way remained forever.

Since then, things are changing. The genre of history has accepted many possible varieties. In addition to the conventional archival documents, Historians are now going for a series of non-conventional sources like music, literature or fictions, traditions, artifacts and sample surveys etc. New areas of research have been opened up, such as the history of cultural productions, visual, audio and performing arts. More and more works are being done on novel aspects of Indian History, formerly unnoticed by historians. In this new process, the boundaries between history and philosophy or between history and music or other disciplines are often blurred or merged together. But, even then, the multiple representations of the past are never to be narrowed down, only the historian has to be more cautious to maintain the flexibility as well as the rigidity of the discipline.

Thanks to Dr. Avijit Ghosh from all these perspectives. We all know that Indian Classical Music has always occupied a central place in the imagination of Indians. But excepting few researches, no good historical work has been made to delineate the musical happenings of the past. The reason behind this lies in the fact that the 'Gharana' or Indian classical musical tradition seemed to be oral, mostly hereditary and individualistic (Guru - Shishya parampara based) in its essence. There were elements of privacy and patronage secrecy and divinity, retained and preserved in this heritage, which did not match with the Eurocentric historian's story - telling of today. On the contrary, the vernacular tradition of history in India was not necessarily prosaic, or even written. Rabindranath Tagore had often regarded his *'Katha'* (poetic ballads) as better histories than *'Kahini'* or prosaic stories. However, as far as the history of classical music is concerned, the best methodology would be a fusion between the empirical and the oral, a combination of the history of music with musicology.

Though not a professional historian, Dr. Avijit Ghosh has experimented with this methodology, in his book in the best possible way. As a historian he had cited references from all the available written sources; and as a performing artist, he has expanded his space of research through his knowledge of performing arts. He had also utilized his musical pavilion by appropriating relevant pictures, interviews and field surveys from experts.

The Chapters have a multiplicity. The first chapter deals with the origin and development of the Sarod. The debates regarding the Hindu or Islamic identity of Sarod have been discussed with a secular, dispassionate rationality. The meaning of the word Sarod, the history of the emergence, either from the Rabab tradition of Central Asia or the Kachhapi Vina of the ancient Hindu tradition are noted with particular reference to all the relevant opinions. We get the story of the gradual evolutions and ultimate modernization of this classical instrument in the hands of Ghulam Ali Khan, who invented the modern Sarod with the qualities of both Sursingar and the Rabab of the Seniyas. This book has a macro-level span in the sense that it is composed in the wider terrain of Indian classical music, on which very little historical work has been done.

At the same time, in the micro-level, Avijit has concentrated on the history of a particular classical instrument i.e. Sarod of which he is a maestro. And that too, he has done by highlighting the contribution of the Seniya Maihar Gharana. In this particular field Acharya Baba Alauddin Khan Sahib, the founder father himself is a history and a living legend.

The Second Chapter gives a detailed narration of the Gharana, with the Baba as the epicenter and his illuminating disciples like Ustad Ali Akbar Khan, Pandit Ravi Shankar, Annapurna Devi, Pandit Nikhil Banerjee and others as the other illuminating planets of music. This chapter is unique of its kind for its extensive wide span starting from the Baba and ending with young stars like Tejendra Narayan Majumdar and Partha Sarathy Choudhury. The chapter is the link between the past, the present and the future.

The third and fourth chapters are perfectly technical keeping in touch with Musicology. The third is on the structural patterns and development made on Sarod in the Seniya_Maihar Gharana. The fourth is written on the technique of the Sarod. The pictures of the instrument including the hands which will play on it give a minute detail of the present development of the instrument. These are very useful particularities for the future learners, and further researchers along this line.

The author writes further about the contribution of the Seniya Maihar Gharana in his fifth chapter. Here we get the instances of Baba Allauddin's unique system of training. The originalities of Ustad Ali Akbar Khan and Pandit Ravi Shankar are also recorded with reference to the lists of their disciples or Sishyas who are continuing the tradition.

The final chapter notes the interviews of some eminent musicians like Pandit Kumar Prosad Mukherjee, Meera Banerjee, Kalyani Roy, Buddhadev Dasgupta etc. of other Gharanas. This sample survey on the opinions about the contribution of the Seniyas Maihar Gharana is really significant, as it brings the impartial visions of the experts in various fields and widens the horizons of the readers. The conclusion is also very open ended, as it leaves much scope for further research on the theme. The bibliography is extensive and the author is frank and confident in his hypothesis.

A brilliant performer of Sarod, Avijit Ghosh has never planned to write a super refined analysis along the lines of a mainstream historians. The book is a wonderful Meta narrative, with its allegiance to facts and descriptions. In spite of the global prestige and fame of Indian classical music, it is really unfortunate that not a large number of history writing to limelight the silenced, yet musical memories of the past. I wish him success and hope that researchers of similar kind will be done in future.

Dr. Mohua Sarkar
Professor of History
Jadavpur University.

ACKNOWLEDGEMENTS

I would like to acknowledge the individuals and institutions, that helped me to make this work possible. I offer my deepest sense of gratitude to my revered teacher and supervisor Dr. Goutam Nag, Reader and Head of the Department of Instrumental Music, Rabindra Bharati University, Kolkata, for his help and guidance at every stage.

To my respected Gurus and Guruma, I owe the continued inspiration for performance and study in this field. The profundity of their musical knowledge is beyond the words, and I can only attempt to be worthy of their teachings.

Many other artistes and scholar - musicians, whom I had approached for information were open and generous. Shri Shyamal Nath shared his knowledge and experience over many meetings. Ustad Aashish Khan and his sister Smt Ameena Perera were generous with their time and provided a detailed history of their family's Sarod lineage. Shri Birendranath Banerjee, the seniormost disciple of the Maihar School of Music, had provided his valuable time in giving me information about Acharya Baba Alauddin Khan Sahib and his method of teachings at Maihar. I am indeed thankful to flautist Shri Nityanand Haldipur for giving me valuable information on Late Pandit Pannalal Ghosh. Shri Supriyo Banerjee and Shri Nityanand Haldipur were both kind enough in providing me with the names of the disciples of Smt Annapurna Devi.

I owe a lot to Smt. Usha Majumdar for providing me with rare photographs taken by Late Shri Shelly

Majumdar. I am indebted to Shri Somjit Dasgupta for providing me valuable information and photographs of various types of Sarods.

I owe a lot to Late Hemen Sen and Shri Dulal Chandra Kanji (eminent Sarod craftsmen) for providing me valuable information on the structural developments made on the Sarod in this Gharana.

Late Pandit Kumar Prosad Mukherjee, Smt. Meera Bandhyopadhyay, Pandit Buddhadev Dasgupta, Surashree Kalyani Roy, Pandit Anindo Chatterjee were very generous with their time and were kind enough to express their opinion about the contribution of the Seniya Maihar Gharana towards music as well as towards the development of the Sarod.

I am indebted to my parents Shri Arun Kumar Ghosh and Smt. Jyotirmoyee Ghosh. Without their blessings I would not be able to complete my work. I am thankful to my in-laws, wife Gargi and daughter Prerana for their support and inspiration. I also thank my sisters Smt Sudeshna Ghosh and Smt Subhamita Chaudhuri for helping me in arranging and editing the manuscripts. I am also thankful to my best friend Dr. Subhasis Biswas for his sincere effort in bringing out the thesis in book form without his help it wouldn't have been possible. I owe a lot to my dear students who learn Sarod from me for their continuous support and cooperation.

I am blessed to have Didi (Dr. Mohua Sarkar and Dada (Shri Sudipto Sarkar) for their supports in reviewing and especially didi's foreword in this book. Then I thank Shri Pallab Purakayastha for typing the manuscripts.

Finally, I pay tribute for all those who supported me and assisted me. Many other persons whom I met and talked with were generous, and I shall always remember their warm cooperation.

Avijit Ghosh

1

General History of the Sarod and its Evolution

1.1 Different Opinions about the Origin of the Sarod

There are various beliefs regarding the origin of the Sarod. As it is a very ancient, traditional instrument. In order to understand the evolutionary history of the instrument the different opinions of eminent musicians and musicologists are to be considered. The views of some of the well-known musicians and musicologists are mentioned below.

"Dr. A. Rashid (1969) mentions that the word Sarod is found in medieval usage. He says that, among the other musical modes or notes Amir Khusrau mentioned Usul-I-Fakhta, Rihawi, Hussaini and Sarod. The term Sarod was also used to denote musical modes or melodies or song (Sarod) but not any musical instrument in particular.

In *Historical Development of Music,* Swami Prajnanananda mentions that a Sarod like instrument is seen in some of the Champa Caves in Madhya Pradesh.

Another book by him *A Historical Study of Indian Music* also gives sketches of a Sarod type Veena in the Gandharva Caves of 1st and 2nd Century and those of Amravati of 2nd - 3rd Century B.C.

Dr. S.K. Banerjee Musicologist from Madhya Pradesh suggests in one of his articles that the ancient instruments Godha Veena. Vipanchi Veena have to be taken into consideration in connection with the origin of Sarod. Godha Veena gets its name because it has the parchment of Godha or Iguana. The archeological findings or Rupar (2000 B.C.) sculptural representations of Gandhava (6th Century B.C.) in Maharashtra of the 1st and 2nd Century B.C. all indicate the existence of instrument resembling the modern Sarod with 3 or 4 strings. Dr. Banerjee also mentions that the archaelogical research suggests the existence of the Scrod like instrument in China, Russia and parts of Asia.

Quoting from Millard's *The Artists of Unknown India* Goswami says that the tribes of Deccan are said to have possessed a type of Guitar which looked like a combination of the Veena and Sarod.

The Kabuli Rabab Players, who settled in India around 2nd half of the 19th Century claim to be the inventors of the Sarod. McNeil maintains that two different Kabuli Rabab players independently claim to have invented the Sarod and their claims have been endorsed by their descendents and disciples especially Niyamatuallah Khan. Both the claimants independently attempted to modify the Kabuli Rabab [Fig. 1.1]. McNeil then stated that Niyamatullah Khan added the metal fingerboard and Gulam Ali Khan incorporated some features of Surshringar as well. Late Pandit Radhika Mohan Moitra seems to support McNeil's view point.

While history is hazy, it seems that the changes in Kabuli Rabab occurred around 1860 and that they were influenced by instruments used for playing music in the Seniya style. And it was around this time when efforts were started to bring Sarod to its present state of sophistication, improving its predecessors namely the instruments Indian Rabab or the Seniya Rabab" [Fig. 1.2]. "The newly emerging Sarod in many ways resembled the Kabuli Rabab, the Seniya

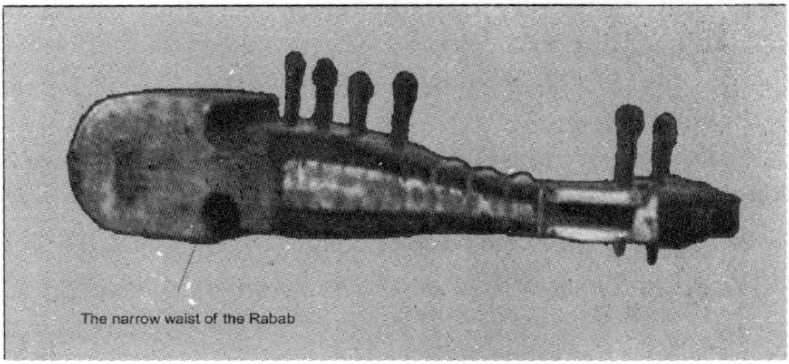

Fig. 1.1. There is evidence that the Kabuli Rabab may be the progenitor of a number of Indian instruments. The Sarod and the Sarangi are the ones most commonly attributed to this instrument. The narrow "waist" in the middle of the Rabab is an indication that the instrument at some time was played with a bow.

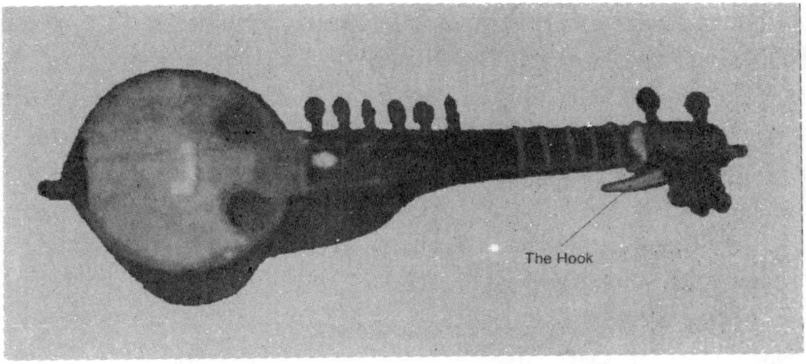

Fig. 1.2. Seni Rabab was an instrument that was very popular during the Moghul period. The main distinguishing characteristics was the large hook at the back of the head of the instrument, used to sling it over the shoulder, allowing it to be played while marching in processions. The Seni Rabab is virtually extinct today.

Source: http://chandrakantha.com/articles/indian_music/rabab.html : Fig. 1.1
http:// www.chandrakantha.com/articles/indian_music/seni.html : Fig. 1.2

Rabab and the Surshringar. At first glance, these might be mistaken for the same instrument because of their pear-shape fretless finger-board and parchment covered faces (resonance box).

Bharat Muni in his *Natyashastra* describes an instrument called Chitra Veena thus :

Sapta-tantri Bhavecchitra Vipanchi Navatantrika
Vipanchi Konavadya Syat Chitra Changuli Vadana.

NATYASHASTRA 29/114

Pandit Lal Mani Mishra in his book *'Bharatiya Sangeet Vadya'* states that old form of Rabab, Surshringar and Sarod can be traced to Chitra Veena. During the medieval period the Chitra Veena was called Rabab which was modified and made into Surshringar by Jafar Khan. Generally it is seen that Rabab, Surshringar and Sarod belong to the same family of instruments, whose origin is the Chitra Veena" (Khan, A., 1991)[1].

According to Dr. Suneera Kasliwal's book "Classical Musical Instruments", the word 'Sarod' (song or melody) belongs to Persian origin. Some scholars suggest that the word might also be used to denote some type of musical instrument of the medieval period. However there is no consensus on this point. According to Allyn Miner, one scholar has suggested that in order to distinguish the Afghani Rabab [Fig. 1.3] from the Seniya Rabab, the players of Afghani Rabab started calling it *Sarod.* By joining various links it can be concluded that the instrument Sarod is an outcome of the combination of the structural characteristics of the Seniya Rabab, Afghani Rabab and the Sursingar. However, if we take into consideration tuning and the Seniya Rabab, one is tempted to contend that the insrument is indigenous. The invention of the Sarod is claimed by the descending students of the two Afghani gharanas of Sarod players. The Afghani rabab was initially a martial instrument which came to India with the Afghani soldiers

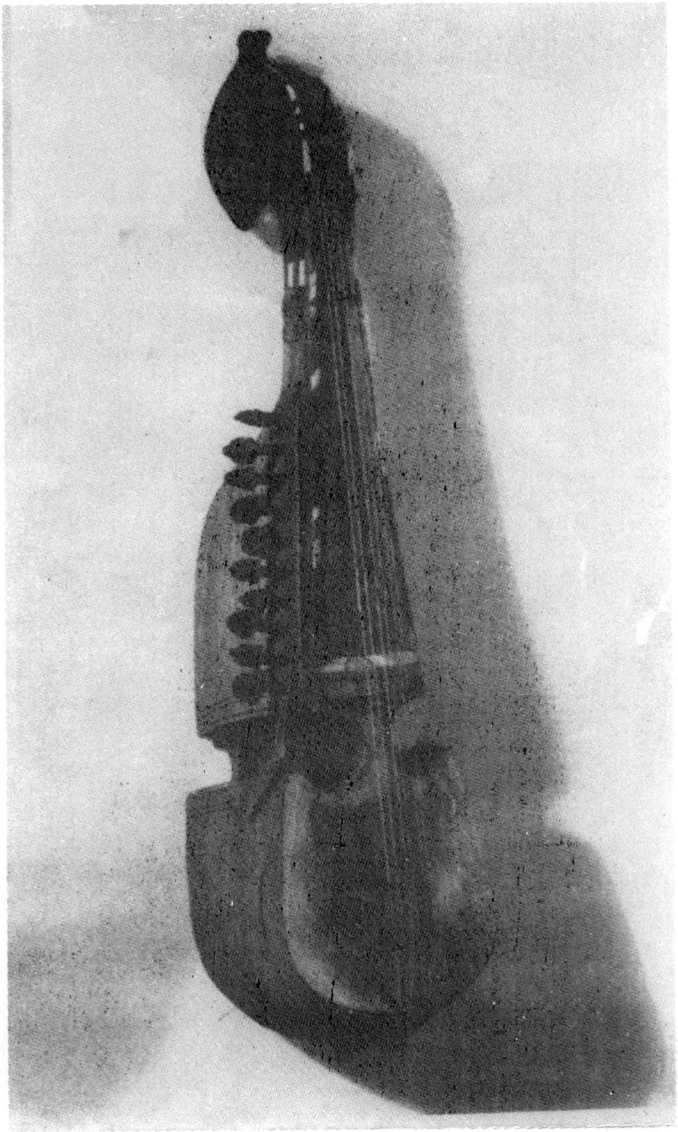

Fig. 1.3. An Afghani - style Rabab.

Source: Miner, A. (1997).

Fig. 1.4. Rural scene with a player of an unidentified short lute

Source: Miner, A. (1997).

Fig. 1.5. A Mongol chieftain with the Rabab player (c 1600)

Source: Miner, A. (1997).

Fig. 1.6. A Rabab player with a prince and a faqir (c1650)

Source: Miner, A. (1997).

Fig. 1.7. Women playing Rabab and Daff (1785-90)

Source: Miner, A. (1997).

in the sixteenth or seventeenth century. But much before the arrival of this Afghani Rabab, the Seniya Rabab had acquired a higher status and was popular in Indian Music. As McNeil puts in, "There is a little doubt, however, that this instrument (the Seniya rabab) had a well established performance tradition before the arrival of the Afghani rabab in India during the eighteenth century.

Niyamatullah Khan, one of the claimants for inventing the Sarod, became a student of Basit Khan, while the latter was in the services of Wajid Ali Shah in Metia Buruj. Later Niyamatullah Khan moved to Nepal where he served the king for thirty long years. Descendents of his gharana claim that, he was responsible for some of the most vital modifications in the Sarod, such as metal strings and metal plate of the fingerboard. His two sons Karamatullah and Asadullah (better known as Kaukubh Khan), carved out a niche for themselves as renowned in Sarod music in Calcutta. The modifications introduced by Niyamatullah Khan in the existing Sarod during the years 1858-1869, as claimed by his son Karamtullah Khan are documented in his book "Israr-I-Karamat Urf Naghmat-I-Niyamat and Risala Sitar (1908)" (Kasliwal, S. 2001)[2].

Another claimant, an Afghani Rababiya (Rabab player), Gulam Ali, was the grandson of Bandagi Khan an Afghani Rabab player settled at Riwa. Gulam Ali learnt Hindustani Music from the Maharaja of Riwa. He is also said to have studied under Pyar Khan and Jaffar Khan while he was in Lucknow for a short period. Renowned Sarod player Hafiz Ali Khan was a descendent of Gulam Ali.

Musical instruments very similar to Sarod (one of Indian most beloved musical instruments) are shown in old caves, temples, in sculptures and paintings in various parts of India, from at least 200 B.C. [Figs. 1.4, 1.5, 1.6 and 1.7] Even the posture of the musician sitting with the instrument, holding and playing it is very similar to that of the present day posture of the musician with the instrument. Illustrations from early times along with this text amply prove the aforesaid point.

In India many stringed instruments were known as Veena, such as Shat-tantri Veena, Rudra Veena, Kachhapi Veena, Vipanchi Veena, *Chitra* Veena, etc. Some Scholars are of the view that Sarod is the Chitra Veena or Kachhapi Veena of earlier times. The belly of this instrument was probably covered with animal skin. In this connection, a reference from Kalidasa (Circa 450 A.D.) is very important as it throws light on the use of material in the making of this instrument.

The Yaksha says to the cloud messenger in the Meghdoot :

"Aradhyainam Sharavanabhavam devamullanghitadhvam
siddhadvandaih jalakanabhayat vini bhirmukta margah"

MEGHDOOT 1.45

It means :

'Having worshipped Lord Skanda, when you proceed further you will find the siddha couples running away from their paths with their Veenas (Sarods) fearing that, they would go out of tune due to the rain drops falling on their instrument'.

A word regarding the etymology of the word Sarod is called for. It is called 'Swarode' in Bengal, which is another variant of the word 'Sarod'. Both these words are derived from the Sanskrit word 'Svarodaya' meaning the rising of Svara. There is a Sutra in "Kavca Prakash", according to which k g c h j t d p y and v very often disappear if they appear between two vowels. Thus Sarod is made out by dropping v and y in Svarodaya.

From the rich source of visual material in the form of sculpture from Bharut (200 B.C.) and Sanchi (first century B.C.) and Ajanta paintings (475 A.D.) it is established that Sarod was recognized as an instrument in the framework of classical music it had a prominent position in court patronage. It is well known that Eastern Afghanistan comprising Kabul and Kandhar was an integral part of India in ancient times. The Gandhara stone relics shows prevalence of Sarod in that region in the third century A.D., thus the music and musical instruments of the heartland of India reached out to the far - flung areas, where the Indian culture dominated. In the 15th to 18th century in several illustrated manuscripts and miniature paintings representations of an instrument resembling the Sarod are found. This is the Sarod of that period although, later or more developments took place till the present form of Sarod was evolved. In 1988, Museum Rietberg, Zurich published illustrations from the book *"A Janiesque Sultanate Shahnama"* of Circa 1450 A.D., with text by scholar B. L. Goswami, showing a seated female Sarod player. From this publication Dr. Goswami has translated the poem accompanying this illustration as follow : "A full week went by in these joyous celebrations, the sounds of the Sarod and Santoor instruments reverberating through the palace".[3]

In SRA seminar, a paper presented by Smt. Shree Gangopadhyay on 'Sarod', which shows that "the existence of 'Rabab' was first noticed in 'Greece' where it is called as 'Rebet'. At the same time in eastern Europe this instrument was known as 'Rubeba'. In Persia and Arabia, this instrument was played by Bowing stick (Chhadi). But in Middle Asia, this instrument was also be used in 'Afghanistan' and 'Kabul' where it was played by 'Jaya'. In this country this instrument was placed in front of the procession when the kings went for hunting or for a visit to a foreign country. Then this instrument was suspended by the neck and played down, but at that time, it had no classical touch, instead it was used to play the village songs. In Kabul this instrument was known as 'Sharudh'. This was a little bit smaller than the original 'Rabab' and was made by the wood of walnut. The table of Sharudh remained covered with sheet of leather and the plates was made up of wood. The strings of loom are arranged on this plate. This instrument was played by the fingers on the plate and by the help of 'Java'. In the first half of Nineteenth Century, Hayder Ali Khan of Kabul, the father of famous Sarodia Late Ghulam Ali Khan, came to India, along with this 'Sharud' of Kabul. Late Ustad Ghulam Ali Khan modified this instrument to some extent and named it 'Sarod'. In fact the grand father of famous Sarodia Ustad Amjad Ali Khan was the first who introduced the modern Sarod. But regarding this there are many views. According to some authors Asadullah Khan, who is famous as Kukubh Khan, was the first inventor of Sarod. In Nineteenth Century, he was the first who introduced Sarod in Bengal.

As Sarod has been evolved from original Rabab [Fig. 1.8], Sarod has got many similarities with it. Like Rabab it has no *'Parda'* The *Tumba's* of both Rabab and Sarod are made up of woods of *Segun* and *Gambhar*. The opened top of the *Tumba* of Rabab remained covered with sheet of leather, and at the *'tabli'* of Rabab was covered with the skin of Iguana. But at present the *tabli* of Rabab becomes covered with the leather coming from goats, cows or monkeys. No metal string had been used in Rabab. There remains 6 loom strings in the Rabab. But there were some Rababs, which are fitted with 12 to 18 metal strings. On the *tabli* of instrument there remains a *'Sawari '* on which the strings are fitted. One end of the string remained tied up with six *'Khuties'* in the upper end of the Rabab, and the other ends remain tied up with *'Panthi'* at the back of the *tumba*. *Panthi* is made up of bones or horns. The metal string of ancient Swardhad has been arranged in the same fashion as Rabab. The Rabab was tuned by a specific mechanism. Out of the six strings, the first one called as *'Giran'* was tuned to *Rishav* of *Madhya Saptak*, the third quest of Ghulam Bandegi Khan Bangash for something more that resulted in the modification of the Rabab with certain additions – the new element of melody being the high point of change

Fig. 1.8. A Rabab player, Kashmir

Source: Miner, A. (1997)

(largely made possible with a metal chest on the fingerboard along with metal strings instead of gut). And it was this concept of melody which gave the instrument its name Sarod, - being literally a derivation from 'Sarood' meaning melody in Persia. These innovations won Gulam Bandegi Khan Bangash great acclaim which was further perfected by his son Ghulam Ali Khan Bangash" (Gangopadhyay, S., 1991).[4]

In the SRA seminar, a paper on Sarod presented by Ustad Mukhtar Ahmed, through that the word Sarod has come from the Persian word sarood meaning melody. This instrument is usually made of wood called *Segun* or*Tun.* The different parts of Sarood are the drum which is called *Piyala* or *Kund,* and a finger board called plate and the neck called *Sindika.* It is an established fact that sarood has come from the Kabuli Rabab. This instrument came to India with Pathan Soldiers and horse traders belonging to the Bangash clan. History of Sarood is linked to Majaf Ali Khan and Madar Ali Khan. Majaf Ali Khan was a horse trader and Madar Ali Khan held a commission in the cavalry. They settled in Rohitkhand where the pathans were in majority. After settling in India, they decided to learn Indian Classical Music. Since the Rabab was not suited this kind of music, they modified it a little bit. They enlarged the size and did away with the fruits and named it Sarod. (Ahmed, M.,1991)[5].

An instrument similar to the Sarod, the Rabab, was found in the Middle East, as far back as the 10th Century. Although the Arabian Rabab was and still is, a bowed instrument, it was the plucked variety of this lute originating in Persia which found its way into the Sub-continent during the Ghaznavid occupation of Punjab in the 11th Century. While most theory attribute the development of the Sarod to the Rabab, and this is broadly correct, Miner points out the need to differentiate between the various types of Rababs that existed in medieval India. Although, the Rabab was quite popular in the Mughal and other courts and developed into an instrument for dhrupad, this Indian or dhrupad rabab, referred to by McNeil (1983) as the Senia Rabab, was quite different structurally from the Sarod, since it had to large round body, a turned back collar and a tapering neck.

There is reason to believe that the predecessor of the present Sarod was a different instrument, the plucked Afghan Rabab. The Afghan Rabab had a bridge which was designed from 'single' point contact with the string, as is the case of the Sarod. This results in a different quality of sound compared to the Senia Rabab which had a wooden bridge. The Afghan Rabab was a short lute with deep narrow body having an indented narrow waist carved out of a single piece of wood. The instrument had gut strings as well as gut frets. It appears that this Rabab was brought into India by Afghan migrants who settled in the Rohilkhand region around Rampur as was noted by Augstus Willard.

Historical records as well as oral traditions point to the evolution of the Sarod sometime in the early 19th Century. Reference to Sarod players through the use of the term of sarodiya is found in Hakim Mohammed Karam Imam's 'Ma'dan-al-musiqi' published in 1856, where Dahajaudaulah Dhari and Ghulam Ali Dhom are mentioned as sarodiya-s in Wajid Ali Shah's Court. When it comes to the question of the origin of the Sarod, there are two contesting claimant gharanas vying for the credit of fashioning the Sarod. On the one hand, Karamatullah Khan in his 'Najmat Niyamat', also known as 'Israr-e-Keramat', contends that his father Niamutullah Khan designed the Sarod. On the other hand it has also been contended that the Sarod came into existence as a result of modifications made to the Afghan Rabab by Ghulam Bandagi Khan Bangash, a Rabab player of Afghan origin.

The metal finger-board and the metal strings are the two main features that distinguish the modern Sarod from the Afghan Rabab. It appears that the early Sarod played by Ghulam Ali had a wooden finger-board, as he had spent time with Pyar Khan, the inventor of the Sursingar and that metal fingerboard can be attributed to Niamatullah Khan who was a disciple of Basat Khan, Pyar Khan's brother. It was the replacement of the wooden finger-board with the steel which was the final stage that brought the Sarod, as we know it into being. Niamatullah Khan (1816-1911) moved with Wajid Ali Shah to Calcutta in 1858, after the latter was exiled by the British from Awadh and was a well-known Sarod player in musical circles there " (Bagchee, S., 1998)[6].

The early history of the Sarod is more clearly accounted for and far more closely agreed upon the sitar. A few differing theories do exist, however, and the main ones are examined here for the sake of record. S.M. Tagore in the 'Yantra Kosha' attempting to relate all modern instruments to an earlier Sanskrit tradition, calls the Sarod the *Saradiya Vina* (the Vina belonging to the sage Sarada). Later scholars make the same statement, taking it either directly from Tagore or indirectly from the Calcutta tradition that he noticed. Sharadiya is a Vina name found occasionally in Sanskrit drama and poetry, but not in Sanskrit musicological literature. Its characteristics are unknown. Its association with the Sarod is based on an imaginative phonological similarity and has no historical basis.

"The word Sarod or *sarud* was a Persian word for music or singing and may have been a term for a medieval musical instrument as well. The immediate source of the name in India is not certain. Its mention occurs as early as 1830. It is not clear at what point the name Sarod came to be applied to the instrument, since the earliest descriptions show none of the modifications that would distinguish Sarod from the Rabab. Two structural differences are normally thought to distinguish the modern Sarod from Afghani Rabab, the replacement of gut with steel strings, and the covering of the fingerboard with a metal plate. The earliest source that describes Sarod, however report neither of these features. In the "Ma'dan-al- musiqi" it is described as having gut strings. It originated from the Rabab says Karam Imam but is "one and a half in length ("qad men devdha"). As late as 1875 the "Sarmaya -I -Ishrat " describes the Sarod as having four gut strings. There is still no mention of a metal plate. An 1872 drawing in Baden - Powell's "Hand -Book of the Manufactures and Arts of the Punjab" depicting "Sarod or Rabab" indicates no difference. One scholar has the idea that the name was first applied simply to distinguish it from the Dhrubab Rabab.

The "Ma'dan-al-musiqi" and most oral traditions mention a figure, Ghulam Ali Khan, a Rababia, who is the earliest musician associated with the instrument called Sarod. Descendents give him or his brother Murad Ali Khan credit for creating the instrument. Ghulam Ali Khan was the grandson of a Rabab player from Afghanistan, Bandegi Khan. Ghulam Ali lived in Rewa. He learnt Hindustani Music from musicians in the various courts where he lived. He had died before the "Ma'dan al-musiqi" was written, so he apparently lived in the first half of the 19th century. Since Ghulam Ali is the earliest figure associated with the instrument called Sarod, it is likely that he instituted some changes to the rabab and/or called it by the new name.

An 1864 catalogue of musical instruments by Meadows Taylor describes a curious instrument 'Sarrooda', grouped along with the bowed sarangi and cikara but larger and "more powerful" than the sarangi, it was an instrument that could be either bowed or plucked. In Karam Imam's Lucknow the Sarod was a larger version of the Afghani rabab, presumably still with gut strings, wooden fingerboard and sympathetic strings. In 1875 (Delhi) the Sarod had four gut strings and seven bronze *tarab* strings". "Charges were beginning to occur, however this time. In the same year in Calcutta S.M. Tagore describes the Sarod (Sarod or Saradiya

Vina) as having six strings and says that players from time to time choose the used steel or other metal strings instead of gut. The strings are tuned to M,M,S,S,P,P. The two doubled pairs are played as one, an interesting pre-20th century stringing. The sixth string is used for "accompaniment" (*sur yog*) and seems to be a kind of *cikari*. There are seven to eleven *tarab* strings. Tagore comments that it is somewhat harsh, not as sweet sounding an instrument as the been, sitar or rabab. Supporting Karam Imam's note on size, Tagore says the 'Arab Sarod' probably the Afghani Rabab, is somewhat similar than the Indian Sarod. An 1889 Sarod on exhibit in the Metropolitan Museum, New York, with the Tagore Collection and presumable from Calcutta, still has no metal plate". There are six main pegs and places for nine tarab strings. It has a somewhat shallower body than the Rabab also exhibit and is highly ornamented, the entire instrument painted elaborately.

Karamatullah Khan told us that his father, Sarod player Na'matullah Khan, who lived about 1816-1911, instituted the changes that we think of as defining the modern Sarod, [Fig. 1.9 A, B] and identifies a specific time period for the changes his father instituted three changes in the Sarod during the time he was living in Navab Wajid Ali Shah's court-in-exile in Calcutta, from 1858 to 1869. At that time Na'matullah Khan reportedly covered the fingerboard with a brass plate, replaced the gut string with steel ones and removed two gut frets that had been on the rabab. Karmatullah Khan comments that while almost everyone copied father's innovations as he made them, some people replaced the two gut frets, which would not hold on a metal fingerboard, with metal frets. From Tagore's comments it seems that use of metal instead of gut string was a trend not attributable to any person. It is agreed upon, that Na'matullah Khan introduced the metal plate by which the modern Sarod is recognised. Na'matullah Khan's Sarod

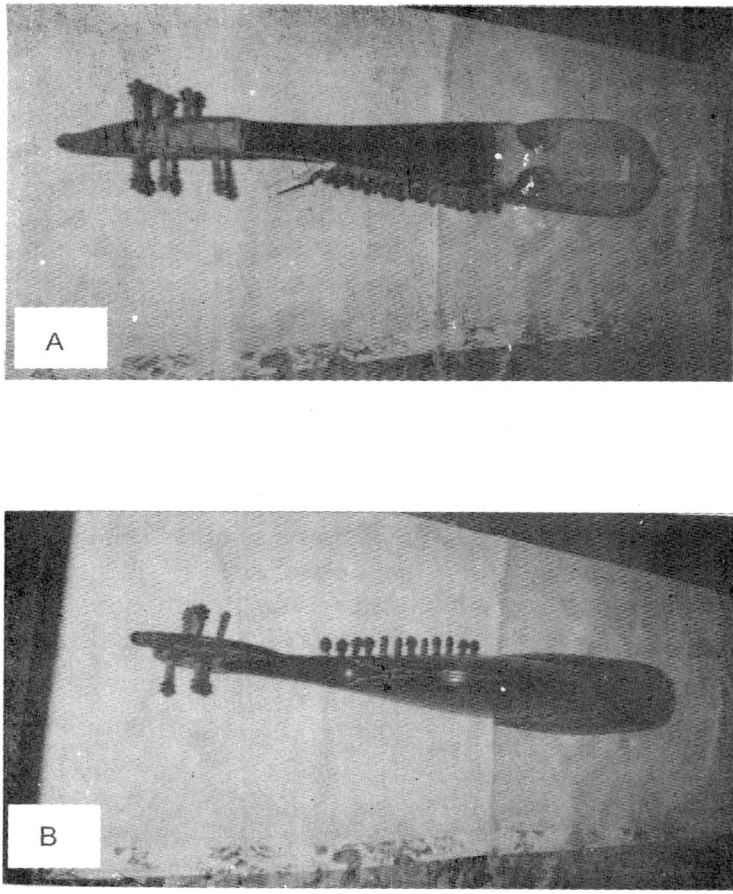

Fig. 1.9. Rabab of Ustad Niyamatullah Khan (1809 - 1902) of Lucknow Gharana, also known as folk Rabab. It is the ancestral instrument of Ustad Niyamatullah Khan. (A) Top view, (B) Bottom view

Source: Somjijit Dasgupta.

as six main strings, one *cikari* string and seventeen *tarabs*. The tuning of the strings is not given but Karamatullah Khan claimed that his father "charged the tuning (that) of the Sarod to make it like that of the sursingar and the (dhrupad) rabab [Fig. 1.10 A, B].

Karamatullah Khan's Sarod is larger than that of his father. It has a more round face, a smaller and rounded waist, a larger and deeper body and a fish-shaped peg box bent to the back. It has six main strings, one *cikari* and fifteen strings whose pegs are in staggered placement in the body, as an modern Sarods. The order peg placement was in a single line. The addition of the *cikari* brought the Sarod to its basic modern form." (Miner, A. 1997)[7].

"The present form of the Sarod was developed about 200-250 years ago in India as adoptations of Rabab, Sursringar and Veena.

Since then the art of Sarod playing, has undergone continuous improvement in the hands of some exceptional and dedicated geniuses and it has now reached a level that seems difficult to improve upon.

It is believed that the most significant predecessor of the modern Sarod is the Rabab, an instrument that originated in the Middle East. The Rabab has a wooden fingerboard and string of catgut and was used mainly as an instrument to accompany military marching bands and marriage processions. The Rabab was already in use in India in the 16 th Century during the reign of Akbar, and the *Akbar–Nama* of the 16th Century traveller Abul Fazal mentioned about several Rabab players in Akbar's court. This Rabab, known as the Seni Rabab, was a large and heavy instrument that had to be supported on the shoulder. The Seni Rabab was later modified by Jafar Khan, one of the descendants of Tansen, by the addition of a metal finger-board, a wooden head, metal strings and a bridge of the Sitar type. This instrument come to be known as Sursringar and was a fore runner of the Sarod.

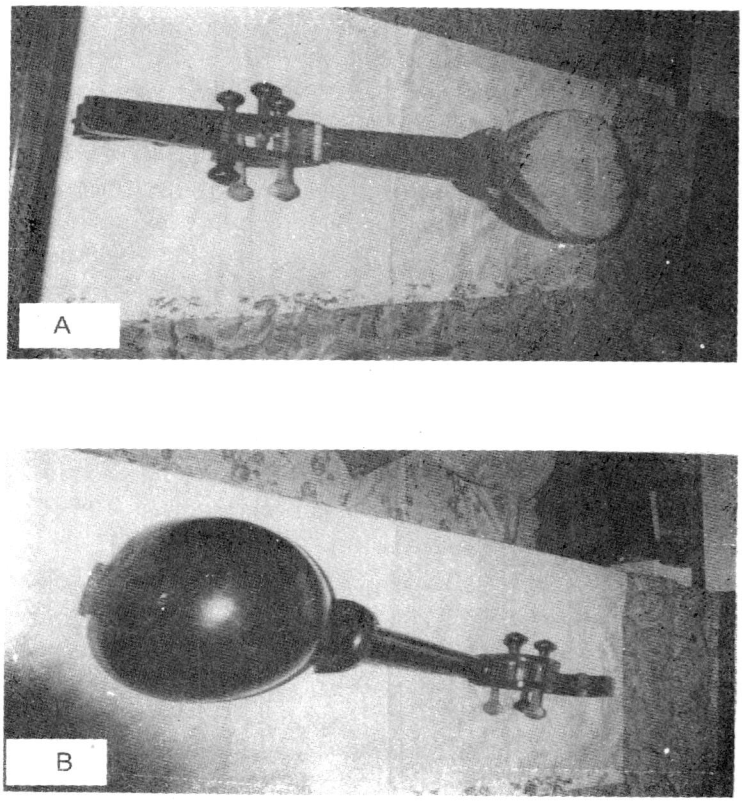

Fig. 1.10. Dhrupadi Rabab of Basat Khan, came to Kolkata in 1857.
(A) Topview (B) Bottom view

Source: Somjijit Dasgupta.

The Sarod, however is closer to the smallar Rabab of Afghanistan and the Rababiyas of Afghnistan are believed to have contributed to its development, after their migration to India. The main Gharana of Afghan origin can be traced back to Ghulam Bandegi Khan Bangash, of Afghanistan, who was a Rabab player, soldier and horse trader, he migrated to India about 300 years ago. He was commissioned as a soldier in the army of Raja Vishwanath Singh of Rewa. Bandegi Khan trained his son Haider Khan and grandson Ghulam Ali Khan in the art of Rabab playing. Ghulam Ali also received musical training from Pyar Khan and the aforementioned Jafar Khan, who were distinguished Rabab players and direct descendents of Tansen.

There are two other district Rababiya families of Afghan origins and it is an important fact that, Enayat Ali and Niyamatullah Khan, who belonged to these respective families were also disciples of Jafar Khan of Seni Gharana, the inventor of the Sursringar. Jafar Khan already used a metal fingerboard and metallic strings in the Sursringar must also have suggested that the Afghan Rabab would profit from a similar modification. The Afghan Rabab had metal finger-board, metallic strings with the addition of the *chikari* and *Tarab*. Thus the Sarod was born. Many more embellishments to the Sarod were made by Ustad Allauddin Khan and his brother Ayet Ali Khan in this century and the modern Sarod has 15 *Tarab* strings, 2 *cikari* strings, 4 main strings, 4 *Thaat* strings tuned to the Raga being played a round head and relatively large resonating chamber. The name Sarod is linked to the Arabic 'Sahrood' or Persian 'Sarood' meaning music, as well as the Sanskrit 'Shorode' ('good noise')[8].

1.2 The Origin of the Pathan Sarod

"Besides the morphological similarities that the Pathan Sarod shares commonly with instruments from the areas to the north-west of India, it can also be said to bear some resemblance to a number of other instruments in India. For example, the ancient Chitra Vina depicted in the reliefs at the Ajanta caves dating from the second century A.D., bears some resemblance to the Sarod. An eminent musicologist the Late Lal Moni Mishra, goes so far to state that the Chitra Vina was the original precursor to the Sarod (1973). Other instruments found in Nepal, South India and Ladakh share same physical characteristics with the Sarod. Given that the Pathan Sarod shares morphological similarities with a number of instruments spread throughout a wide area of South Asia, it would be a difficult and at best inconclusive task to attempt to organologically account for the instrument. Discussion in this section therefore attempts to investigate some aspects of the Sarod's historical background by tracing the etymology of the term Sarod, and examining Pathan sarodiyas own accounts of the origins of instrument.

As early history of the Sarod appears in the Urdu/ Farsi book *Isarare Keramat urf Nagmat Niamat*. This book was written in 1908 by Keramatullah Khan* (1848-1933), a well known Hindustani sarodiya of Pathan descent. The name of the instrument appears in this Urdu book which can be transliterated into Roman script as either 'Sarod or sarud'.

Keramatullah Khan's book short work which provides a description of the instrument and its basic playing technique. As this is not a well-known source, it is worth quoting at length from this text.

Sarod is a Greek word§. The Greeks had an instrument known as the Sarod. Fishew-Ghorus (a Greek) was the inventor of the instrument. No other instrument, before this utilised a structured scale. The present form of the Sarod is not the same as invented by Fishew-Ghorus, but it is certainly there is little difference.

Historians have pointed to the fact that the instrument consisted of seven strings, so the name became sarod perhaps meaning seven. The instrument was invented because Fishew-Ghorus, had said that no other instrument was capable of producing such a complete and harmonious sound. So the instrument evolved from a great deal of though and only emerged slowly over time.

One thousand years ago the Sarod was being used in Afghanistan and was considered both a popular and worthy instrument because its sound was reputed to invoke valour and bravery. Consequently it became the official instrument of the military forces. It came to India about two hundred and fifty years back; but it has always undergone many and varied innovations. Therefore the present day product is the result of hundreds of such changes (1908).

It is not possible, given the scope of this study, to make any comments concerning the contention that the Sarod was invented in Greece. Nevertheless it should be noted that during the colonial period it was common place for Muslim scholars, for whatever reasons to trace matters of social and cultural ancestry to Greece.

Information from Dr. Rashmi Desai (Dept. of Anthropology) Monach University 1990, by A. McNeil.

The point that concerns us here, however is the connection between the Sarod and the Pathan military, an association that is often reiterated by the descendants of other Pathan sarodiyas in India.

Amjad Ali Khan, the well known contemporary descendant of another lineage of Pathan sarodiyas, frequently cites the earlier military role of sarodiyas in interviews and articles. He states that when his principal ancestor migrated to India they not only played the sarod, but was also a *risaldar* (a rank and member of the cavalry), (Malhotra 1973). Iliyas Khan the descendant of a third lineage of Pathan Sarodias states that, apart from being a sarodiya, his main ancestor came to India as a *fauz ka zamadar* (leader of a small army of, usually, mercenaries).

In light of the close, cultural and specifically musical, connection between Pathan and Persian culture, Canton's description of a contemporary genre of Persian music perhaps points to the possibility of an etymological link between Persian music and the Sarod.

Contemporary national, institutional and instructional anthems are called 'soruds'. The 'sorud', unlike 'tasnif' and 'tarane' is meant to be sung by a group, not just by an individual. The connection between this genre and the Pathan musical instrument may at first appear tenuous. However, if the function, which an anthem may serve in a modern political context is considered, i.e. to express some form institutionalised authority and to inspire a patriotic spirit, then it is not unreasonable to suggest that, on the basis of such a function, the music which accompanied military activity prior to modern state formation was the closest equivalent to our contemporary concept of a national anthem. If this was indeed the case, then such a connection could account for the Pathan instrument being named sarod, it was the instrument that played soruds or anthems. Given the communal nature of military activity, it can be said that these anthems would have fulfilled the above criterion that the sorud genre be performed by a group. The musicians that performed these anthems or soruds would be known as 'sarodis'. Later when these musicians became part of Hindusthani music, the term probably became 'sarodiyas'. The eventual change of name from Sarod to Rabab probably occurred in the last half of the nineteenth century, after the British had effectively demilitarised the local armies in and around the Pathan homelands. It would have been at this time that the singing of nationalistic or militaristic anthems would have also disappeared.

It must be conceded that an attempt to link the Persian genre sorud and the Pathan musical instrument Sarod, based solely on the above information, necessarily remains speculative. However, as phonetic variations of Sorud are also to be found in the music culture of geographically and culturally contiguous areas of Iran and the Pathan homelands such as Baluchistan, Sistan, Sindh and the north-western regions of India, additional evidence appears which supports the above hypothesis. Specifically, it is when a number of organologically dissimilar instruments from the north-west of the subcontinent that share a similar name to the Pathan Sarod are examined, that a pattern seems to emerge.

Surod, Sorud, Saroz Sarinda are all names of bowed heart shapes lutes, alternately referred to as double chested fiddles. These smaller instruments are clearly distinguishable from the Pathan Sarod not only on the basis of their dimensions, but by the fact, that they are bowed, while the Pathan instrument is plucked. Whilst the design of these bowed instruments clearly differ from the Pathan Sarod, information in the following passages, nevertheless, suggests that the bowed lutes were also used to accompany forces into battles. Consequently, all these instruments were known by similar name because they shared an identical function on the battle field to accompany military soruds.

The association between the Sarod and the military activity of the Pathans was clearly articulated above by Keramatullah Khan. It is fortunate that some details of this aspect of the performance practice of the above-mentioned bowed lutes are also available. For example, an English traveller Robert Coverte who was met by a group of Baluchi musicians around the Pakthunistan and Baluchistan border in 1610, relates.

Early in the morning and about break of day we met with ten or twelve men playing Fiddles, as if they had come in a friendly manner to welcome us, but indeed they were no better than thieves that intended to rob and pillage us, for by the sun rising we were beset round them and their companions, whose certain number one could not discrene nor know (1987).

The fiddle commonly played by Baluchi musicians is the surod. Therefore, it is reasonable to expect that the filddle played by the musicians from Baluchistan in the above passage was this same instrument. Another bowed double-chested fiddle from the *Sistan* and Baluchistan region of Iran (West of Pakistani Baluchistan) is also known as Surod. This instrument is morphologically identical to its cousins from further east. The same military functions could also be ascribed to the Persian bowed lute known as the Saroz, but which is also referred to as 'geychak'.

It is therefore conceivable that a genre of Persian music, as defined by Caton (1982), may have been used in a general way to describe a nationalistic genre of Persian music, if not the music played in the military tradition of Persia and its culturally contiguous areas. At some stage Sorud probably also came to refer to the instruments and musicians that performed military anthems. The phonetic similarity between the Persian Sarud, the Pathan Sorod, the Baluchi Surod, the Sistani, Sorud, therefore suggests, that the above argument whilst by no means proved, can at present be regarded as a reasonable hypothesis (McNeil, A. 1992)[9].

Shri Ram Avtar Veer says in his text the 'Musical Instruments of India' that "the Sarod is an important string instrument. It is made on the principal of Rabab with some modifications. It is made of wood and measures about 90 to 100 cm. in length. One end of the body of the instrument is round having a diameter about 30 cm. It remains covered with a parchment. Sarod has six main strings of metal including *Chikari* for drone and rhythmic accompaniment. They are fastened to the pegs at the neck end. The fingerboard is covered with a polished metal plate. It has about a dozen sympathetic strings to improve the resonance" (Vir, R.A., 1983)[10].

The history of the Sarod is linked to an instrument of Arab culture called Rabab. In the Arab world Rabab was a bowed lute-type instrument. In Persia, however, Rabab was a plucked lute and it was that form of the instrument that spread widely in the Persian cultural sphere – in present day Afghanistan and in medieval India. Different forms of Rabab are pictured in miniature paintings of the Mughal period (1526-1858). In the oral tradition a particularly large Rabab, used for dhrupad music is traced to the great musician Tansen in the court of Akbar (1556 – 1605). From the time of Akbar and Tansen, the making of music in Mughal courts began to be associated with particular families. Two branches of Tansen's family specialized in different instruments. From his daughter Saraswati, who married a noted been player, Misri Singh, came the Beenkar branch. The descendants of his son, Bilas Khan specialized in playing the Rababs developed by Tansen and became known as the 'Rababiya Gharana' (Ghar meaning 'house' and Gharana meaning 'family' or household). Today the rabab has been replaced by the Sarod in performances of classical music, but most sarod players trace their lineage back to the Rababiya and even back to Afghan Rabab traditions.

It is said that Khan Saheb Asadullah Khan introduced this instrument (the sarod) in Bengal more than a century ago and since then Bengal has become noted for the manufacture and the popularisation of this instrument. In Bengal, Ustad Ali Akbar Khan's father, Ustad Allauddin Khan, developed a style that differs in some ways from the older Sarod styles" (Wade, B.C., 1999)[11].

The paper presented by Pandit Buddhadev Dasgupta at the S.R.A. Seminar on Sarod, shows that "the immediate ancestor of the Sarod is the Afghan Rabab, which had a fretless finger-board of polished wood and catguts for strings". The question "who gave the sarod its present form consisting of steel plates instead of wooden finger-board and metallic strings in place of catguts" is rather hard to answer. The exponents of Gulam Ali's Gharana, strongly claim that he was the person who have the Sarod its present form. But there are counter claims which cannot be brushed aside lightly. To Ustad Niyamatullah Khan of Lucknow Gharana has also been attributed the same credit. To crown everything, both these sarodiyas had taken talim from one or more of the famous Basat Khan -Zafar Khan -Pyar Khan brothers of Tansen's lineage and Zaffar Khan, who was senior to both Niyamatullah Khan and Ghulam Ali Khan had designed the instrument Sursringar from the old Indian Rabab, and its was in the Sursringar that the steel plate and the metal strings were used for the first time. So the idea of these innovations came to him first of all.

The contribution of Baba Allauddin and his brother Ustad Ayet Ali Khan in the shape, size and tonality of today's Sarod is enormous and has to be acknowledged by all. They made the drum larger and round instead of elliptical for better depth tonality and longer *meends,* and added several strings which have effected a great enhancement in the overall musicality of the instrument. Even those who play the old style sarod, have fallen for the larger and rounder drum" (Dasgupta, B. 1991)[12].

The common belief prevalent is that Sarod is a gradually developed form of Rabab and Sursringar. There can be not two opinions about it, but efforts should be made to clarify the various misconceptions about it and a logical conclusion to the problems should be ground by analysis the various texts.

Generally, it is accepted that Sarod is a modern, converted form of Rabab. But from where and did Rabab come originally, from which instrument did it finally evolve, did it come from Afghanistan or Arabia or is India its place or origin?

In a special issue of the SRA journal, Sri Ajay Singh Ravi holds Rudra–Vina to be originator of Sarod (Vol. 9,

No. 1, August 1988 – The Swarode : An Indian Musical Instrument). This view is unacceptable because whereas Rudra–Vina belongs to the category of stick zither, Rabab belongs to the category of lute. In order to establish his theory, the author has overlooked the basic classification or structure of this instrument.

1.3 Rabab

The followers of Tansen believe that this instrument was invented by Tansen himself. This cannot be true because Rabab was in existence and popular in the pre-Tansen period. Because of its popularity, due weightage was given to it by Tansen and his school. Contrary to that, Tansen's Son-in-law, Misri Singh (Naubad Khan) was a Vina player and hence his descendants continued playing Vina along with Dhrupad singing. Hence, their school is known as the 'Seniya Binkar' school of music. This may be one of the reasons why the descendents of Tansen's son adopted Rabab [Fig. 1.11] as their instrument and declared Tansen to be the inventor of this instrument. But this instrument was played even in the period before Tansen. We find references to it in the works of the poets of the pre-Tansen era – Jayasis, Padmavat, Kabir's Sakhiran and Krishna Das's dotar (verses) – Bhai Mardana Singh, the disciple of Guru Nanak Dev, used to sing to the accompaniment of Rabab also.

In 1700 A.D. Ahobala introduced the term Rabab giving it a sanskritzed form in the Sangit Parijata. He placed it in the Tatavadya (Chordo – percussion) category and referred to its seven strings, which were made either of silk or catgut. The first string was tuned to Madhyama svara and the respective ones to consecutive svaras.

Another type of Rabab which was to be found in Sindh, Afghanistan, Kabul [Fig. 1.12] etc. was played by striking a piece of bone of the string. Hence, Chitra–Vina which

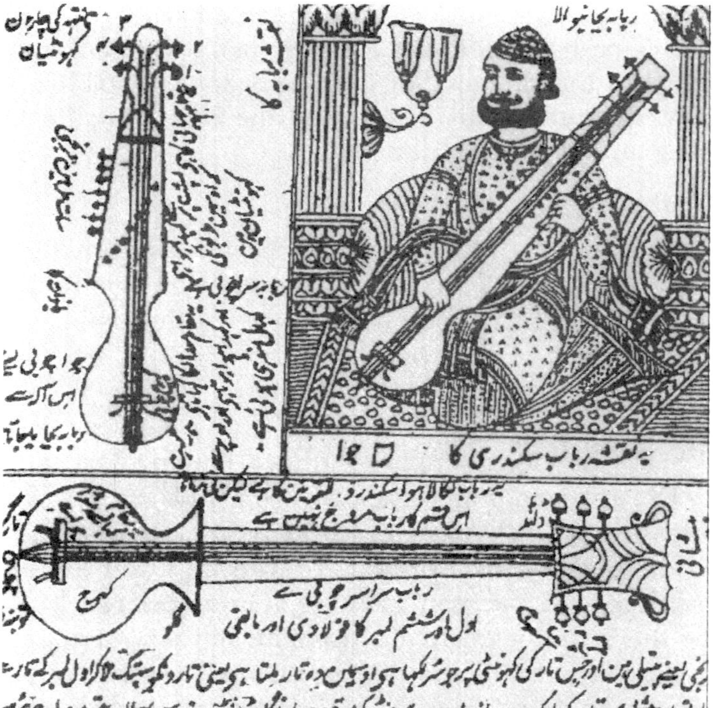

Fig. 1.11. Rabab and Rabab Sikandari

Source: Miner, A. (1997).

Fig. 1.12. Nautch girls and a musician playing the Rabab

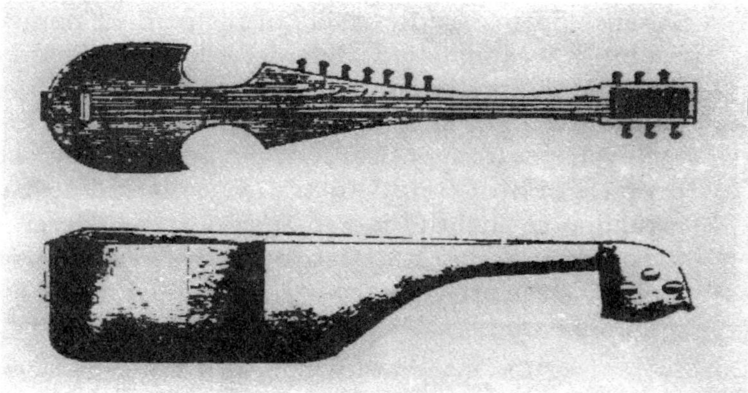

Fig. 1.13. A Rabab in India as drawn by Fetis, F.J., a historian, in 1869

Source: Miner, A. (1997).

was played with the help of the plectrum came to be known as 'RABAB' because of its similar structure. Gradually two types of Rabab came into existence in India also. One was played by plectrum (the Kona) and the other with the help of a bow. The latter is still played in Rajasthan where it is still used as an accompanying instrument in folk music.

The Rabab, played with a plectrum was in popular use among the elite and cultural societies of India [Fig. 1.13] because it originated in India and was widely appreciated. This is the reason why it occupies an important position - as the accompanying instrument in the songs of Guru Nanak Dev (Chakravarty, I., 1991)[13].

1.4 Similarity in Names

(i) "Some scholars hold that Sarod evolved out of the Sharadiya–Vina. But no information of such a Vina is available so far as ancient textual evidences are concerned.

(ii) About 913 A.D. in the Abn-At-Abbas region of Samarkand in middle Asia, an instrument named Shahrud' was invented, Reference to Sarod is to be found in the pre-Indian literature of Iran. B.C. Deva hasn't given any textual evidence in support of his theory, hence it is not clear how the development and propagation of Sarod in India is related to the invention of Shahrud in Samarkand. . The reference to Sarod in literary texts cannot be the sole point on which we can arrive to the conculsion that it was the origin of Sarod.

(iii) According to Dr. Dinesh Chandra Gupta, the term 'Sarod' has its origin in the Arabian Word 'Sah-rud' or 'Sarod' which means 'Music'. The absence of jod string (the sound of tonic note) in Indian Sarod proves that it either originated from the 'Zither' (or Zider) of Afghanistan or the Shah-rud of Arabia. (Sarod ki Utpatti - Dinesh Chandra Gupta.)

(iv) Ustad Amjad Ali Khan, in a journal published in memory of Ustad Hafiz Ali Khan, says that the term 'Sarod' as a distorted form of the Persian 'Sarod' which means *mauisqi naghma, tarannum.*

(v) The modified form of Shahrud was termed as Rabab in Afghanistan. In other words, it can be said that the shahrud of Arabia and Rabab of Afghanistan together form the Rabab of India. Today, the Sarod, which is popular all over India is modified form of the Rabab of Afghanistan. This view of Dr. Dinesh Chandra Gupta is not acceptable.

Even if we accept that the term 'Sarod' is a distorted form of the Persian term 'Shah-rud' or 'Sarud', does it prove that the Indian Sarod came into existence in the 10th century? There is no mention of Sarod in Capt. Willard's book, "Treatise of Music of Hindustan". Written in the 19th century and in Madanul Mausiqi (1856) of Mohammad Karam Iman which underlines the fact that this instrument was not invented in India till then. After sometime, the Surasingara was invented by Zafer Khan. Hence, till the end of the 19th Century, 'Sarod' finds no mention as an instrument.

The argument of Dr. Gupta after the modification of the form and structure of Shah-rud, it came to be known as Rabab in Afghanistan, is also not acceptable.

This new theory can be said to be a mere hypothesis. On one hand, he holds the term 'Sarod' to evolve from Shahrud and on the other hand, the instrument Rabab to evolve from Shah-rud. As said earlier, the form of Rabab which was played with a Kona, was prevalent in India during ancient times under the name of Chitra Vina while the Arabian Rabab was played with the help of a bow.

Though the term 'Sarod' with reference to an instrument did not exist during the time of Akbar the term was not wholly unknown, the meaning also resembled that of

'Shahrud or Sarud, i.e. music, tarannum, naghma. There was a musician in the court of Akbar, Sarod Khan who hailed from Gwalior. This proves that the term 'Sarod' meaning music, was in common usage in those days. Though the term 'Sarod' is mentioned in Akbarnama and Ain-I-Akbari, there is no reference to the instrument 'Sarod'. Thus, it is an established fact thate Sarod is the last link in the chain of Rabab and Sursingara. There is a close resemblance in their shape and structure (Chakravarty, I., 1991)[14].

1.5 Other Views about Sarod

(i) Pt. Jotin Bhattacharya has forwarded two views about the origin of Sarod in his "Ustad Allaudin Khan and his music" – Firstly, Ghulam Ali Khan Bangash, who came to India from Kabul with his father is the inventor of Sarod. Secondly, it is related to the Seniya gharana.

(ii) Ghulam Ali Khan Bangash converted the Afghani Rabab into Sarod.

(iii) According to Dr. Sushil Kumar Chaubey, Ghulam Ali Khan was a resident of Kabul. He was held to an artist of eminance and a keen researcher of Sarod.

(iv) Dr. Paranjape holds that in the present century, the credit for popularising this instrument (Sarod) goes to Haider Ali Khan, who brought it from Kabul. His son was Ghulam Ali.

(v) Sarod is a popular concert instrument in India today. The sarod is a variant of the Afghan Rabab.

(vi) Ghulam Bandagi Khan, the forefather of the famous Sarod player late Hafiz Ali Khan, came to India for horse-trading. He received great encouragement from the Rewa Naresh, Vishwanth Singh. It was he, who converted the Rabab into the present Sarod.

(vii) According to Shri Ajay Singha Ray "the famous swarode player Ustad Hafiz Ali Khan of Gwalior used to claim that this Ghulam Ustad Ali Khan of the court of Nawab of Oudh, his grandfather Ustad Haider Ali Khan were one and the same person.

(viii) Most of the scholars accept Rabab as originator of Sarod.

(ix) Different scholars in their respective works have given credit to either Ghulam Bandagi Khan or Ghulam Ali Khan or Haider Ali Khan as the inventor of Sarod. (Chakravarty, I., 1991)[15].

1.6 Conclusion

After making a detailed and critical analysis of the fact mentioned above, we come to the following conclusions :

(i) Ghulam Bandagi Khan recieved formal training in the modified Rabab and the Afghan Rabab.

(ii) Sarod was invented after sursingar.

(iii) Sarod has the characteritics of both sursringar and Rabab.

(iv) Rabab is made out of a hollow stick. Its ground is made of wood and the tabli (resonator) is framed with leather. It has six strings made of catgut.

(v) Zafar Khan the descendant of Vilas Khan, Youngest son of Tansen, is considered to be the inventor of sursringar. During the monsoon, the tabli (resonator) which was framed with animal skin, used to get moist and the quality of resonance diminished. Thus, the tabli was not made of wood and the sthana or part where the instrument was played was plated with a bright sheet of iron or steel. The catgut strings were replaced by steel and brass ones. It brought a remarkable change in the tonal quality and resonance of the instrument.

(vi) Sarod unites the characteristics of both the instruments viz. Rabab and Sursingar. The statement of Dr. Lal Mani Mishra seems logical. Since the tabli

> was made of wood instead of leather, the size went on increasing, with the result that it became inconvenient for the players to place it in their legs. Hence, keeping in fact the other qualities of the sursringar, the practice of framing the tabli with leather and playing was again started. This new form of Sursringar was called Sarod ..... With the emergence of Sarod and the excellence of its quality, the popularity of Rabab and Sursingar started waning and gradually disappeared.

Thus, if it is accepted that Ghulam Ali Khan as the inventor of Sarod, it should also be apprehended that he united the qualities of both sursingar (invented by his teacher, Zafar Khan) and the Rabab (of the Seniyas, taught to him by his Ustad Zafar Khan) and succeeded in inventing a remarkable instrument which was named 'Sarod' signifying music or tarannum. This remarkable event took place after the completion of Mohammaed Karam Imam's book, because Capt. Willard (mid 19th Century) fails to mention Sarod along with other instruments of that period. Hence, it should be accepted that Sarod came into existence either by the end of the 19th Century or the beginning of the 20th Century. (Chakravarty, I., 1991)[16].

References

1. Khan, Aashish. Ustad (1991): 'Sangeet Research Academy Seminar on Sarod', Western Region, Bombay, pp. 17-24.
2. Kasliwal, Suneera Dr. (2001): Classical Musical Instruments, published by Rupa and Co. pp. 153-161, 166 -175.
3. http://www.divinesarod.com/sarod.html
4. Gangopadhyay, Sree (1991): 'Sangeet Research Academy Seminar on Sarod', Western Region Bombay, pp. 50- 57.
5. Ahmed, Mukhtar Ustad. (1991): 'Sangeet Research Academy Seminar on Sarod', Western Region, Bombay, p. 58.
6. Bagchee, Sandeep. (1998): NAD - Understanding Raga Music, Eeshwar Publications, Mumbai, pp. 261 - 223.

7. Miner, Allyn (1997): Sitar and Sarod in the 18th and 19th Centuries, Performing Art Series, Volume VII, published by Motilal Banarsidass Publishers Pvt. Ltd. Delhi, pp. 60 - 69.

8. http://www.aoe.vt.edu/~boppe/MUSIC/GHAR/sarod.html

   Belonged to Lucknow Gharana Descendent of Niamatullah Khan (of Seminar on Sarod organised by ITC (15th December, 1991 p. 49).

   McNeil, Adrian: 'Sarodiyas in Hindustani Music' Part 2, p. 158.

9. McNeil, Adrian (1983): The Emergence of the Sarod in Hindustani Music, unpublished PhD thesis submitted to Dept. of Music, Monash University.

10. Vir Ram Avatar (1983): Musical Instruments of India (History and Developments), Pankaj Publications, New Delhi, pp. 61 - 62.

11. Wade, Bonnie. C (1999): Music in India (The Classical Traditions), Monohar Publishers, New Delhi, pp. 98 - 101.

12. Dasgupta, Buddhadev. Pt (1991): 'Sangeet Research Academy Seminar on Sarod', Western Region, Bombay, pp. 37- 41.

13. Chakraborty, Indrani Dr (1991): 'Sangeet Research Academy Seminar on Sarod', Western Region, Bombay, pp. 2–16.

14. Chakraborty, Indrani Dr (1991): 'Sangeet Research Academy Seminar on Sarod', Western Region, Bombay, pp. 2–16.

15. Chakraborty, Indrani Dr (1991): 'Sangeet Research Academy Seminar on Sarod', Western Region, Bombay, pp. 2–16.

16. Chakraborty, Indrani Dr (1991): 'Sangeet Research Academy Seminar on Sarod', Western Region, Bombay, pp. 2–16.

2

The Gharana

2.1 Life and Times of Acharya Baba Allauddin Khan

"Allauddin Khan nick named 'Alam' was one of the many sons born to Sodu Main and Harasundari in circa 1871 on *Mahashaptami* day in Shibpur Village of Comilla District in East Bengal.

Sodu Mian was an amateur Sitarist, a disciple of Kasem Ali Khan who was the maternal uncle of Ustad Wazir Khan [Fig. 2.1] of Rampur. Sodu Mian's second son Fakir Aftabuddin, [Fig. 2.2] (an ascetic), was an ardent devotee of Goddess Kali, and lived in a cave near their home. Aftabuddin was gifted singer and musician. He could proficiently play many instruments, like Harmonium, Flute, Pakhawaj, Tabla, Dotara and the Clarionet.

During his childhood, little Alam listened continuosly to his father's sitar and brother's musical renderings. Many ascetics visited Fakir Aftabuddin. They preached and practised various religious rites intermingled with mystic music. Alam could not resist listening to them time and again. That stirred a new musical realization in his young mind. Little Alam was neither interested nor attentive to regular studies, he often visited the Shiva Temple in his village and witnessed Hindus and Muslims paying their respectful offering to the deity. Alam was greatly influenced by these religious rites, and by the ascetics who associated with his brother.

Fig. 2.2. Fakir Aftabuddin, Baba Allauddin Khan Sahib's brother and Guru with the Dotara.

Source: Ruckert, G. (1991) .

Fig. 2.1. Mohammad Wazir Khan of Rampur gharana, Guru to Allauddin Khan Sahib, last of the great Seni Beenkars who traced their blood descent from Tansen.

Source: Ghosh, A. (1990).

Fakir Aftabuddin was at that time learning the Tabla and Pakhawaj from eminent masters. Soon Alam's teachers complained that he played truant from school. One day Sodu Mian actually caught Alam unawares playing the Tabla with a sadhu (Monk) sage accompanying him on the Sitar. Sodu Mian returned home told his wife not to reprimand the boy and to allow him to continue his natural inclination for music. But Harsaundari had a fiery temper, she tied the boy up three days without food. This was the limit of endurance for sensitively disposed Alam. Finally, he decided to run away from home in search of music at the tender age of eight.

From Shibpur Allauddin Khan arrived at Narayangunj to join a group of ministrels where the instrument Dhol, an indigeneous Bengali drum was frequently played by them. Travelling along with these musicians Allauddin Khan reached Dacca. He learnt to play the dhol with great ardour. The ministrels played with Jatra Group. Allauddin Khan learnt to play some typical Jatra instruments like the Harmonium, Tabla, Clarionets Trumpet, Pakhawaj and Dhol. Meanwhile Sodu Mian's family was unaware of Alam's whereabouts. They tried to locate him and finally gave up search and hope too.

From Dacca Allauddin reached Calcutta. Disillusioned, he roamed aimlessly in the big cruel city. The very first day, after a day's fast, he drank water from Ganga being extremely thirsty. To his surprise the water tasted saltish. On the following day, Allauddin, feeling totally lost, and was on the verge of breaking down. He did not know where to turn and what to do. A Sadhu near the river told him to take a dip in the water and proceed straight ahead. Allauddin following the directed path, arrived at an open eating house for the poor. There, he was allowed one free meal a day.

During at night, Allauddin slept on the verandah of a house. Next day he awoke and found to his dismay that the bundle of clothes and a few rupees that he possessed were stolen. But a kind hearted Doctor Kedarnath, hearing the lad's plight and ambition took him to Nulo Gopal, the state musician of Maharaja Jyotindra Mohan Tagore of Pathuriaghata.

Gopal Chandra Chakraborty alias Nulo Gopal was one of the foremost contemporaries in Dhrupadas. His right hand was out of shape because of paralysis. He was an orthodox Brahmin. Being a Muslim, Allauddin took a pseudonym, Prasanna Biswas. He was afraid that he would be thrown out if Nulo Gopal found out his real identity. Thus began Allauddin's initial training. Nulo Gopal taught him sargam for almost seven years alongwith it three hundred sixty *paltas*. Then death claimed him. But by this time Allauddin's musical sense had grown to such an extent, that he could notate anything that he heard, either in his mind or on paper.

After Nulo Gopal's deah Allauddin was left without a Guru. During this time he took up an assignment at Girish Theatre. It was for a paltry sum of one rupee. This time also Allauddin joined under a pseudonym. Allauddin was introduced to Swami Vivekananda's brother a musician and composer, Habu Dutta. He was well conversant with Indian and Western music and conducted Chamber Orchestra. This enabled and inspired Allauddin to form his own Maihar Band later with orphan children. He was a zealous student and learnt violin, from an Anglo - Indian gentlemen named Mr. Robert Lobo (conductor of the Eden Gardens Orchestra) and a along with this mridanga and tabla from Anandobabu. Allauddin also learnt to play shehnai, nakara and tikara wind instruments from Hazarilal Ustads of Mechua Bazar.

In the mean time Fakir Aftabuddin found out his younger brother at a concert and compelled him to return home. There was much rejoining in the family though it was short lived. To put a stop to all his endeavours.

Allauddin [Fig. 2.3] was betrothed to Madan Manjari [Fig. 2.4]. But Allauddin's inveterate passion for music started beckoning him. This fascination made him run away from home again. In his quest, he left his young bride who was unaware of this act. Allauddin was concious that his pursuit was incomplete. He travelled to the great connoisseur of music, Zemindar Raja Jagat Kishore Acharaya who found young Allauddin a keen and enthusiastic learner and recommended him to the renowned sarod player Ahmed Ali, who at the request of the Raja and also seeing the talent in the young man, took Allauddin as his disciple.

The music teachers make their students do all sorts of household chores and adamant as he was to learn music, Allauddin never wavered from doing all odd domestic jobs for Ahmed Ali, he found time to learn fast and practise vigrously. After a couple of years while he was practising to play the Aalap, Ahmed Ali returned home unexpectedly, and was amazed to find his student, practising the secret Aalap in his individual style. The Ustad was so enraged that he almost threw Allauddin out of the house, because like most Ustads Ahmed Ali stressed that certain things were not meant to be passed on to outsiders. These were strictly for the nearest kith and kin. But then anger soon gave way to affection. He advised Allauddin that he had learnt enough and should go out in to the world and be on his own, as the saying goes, *'Sikkha, Dikkha, Parikha'*.

Merely by Allauddin's sheer dedication and perseverance, Ahmed Ali then continued teaching him seriously the style of his tradition. Allauddin accompanied him on concert tours to various cities. Ahmed Ali was addicted to drugs and alcohol. Aware of the bad habit of his master, Allauddin stored away his entire earnings without his knowledge, lest he should spent all the amount on drinks and drugs. Thus he amassed quite a large sum of money over the long period while accompanying Ahmed Ali to various concerts.

Fig. 2.3. Acharya Baba Allauddin Khan Sahib.

Fig. 2.4. Smt. Madina Manjari, Acharya Baba Allauddin Khan Sahib's wife.

Source: Ruckert, G. (1991) : Fig. 2.5 ; Ghosh, A. (1990) : Fig. 2.6

One day in Rampur, Ahmed Ali's paternal grandmother told Allauddin that they felt that his training was incomplete. It was suggested that he should seek and gain more knowledge from another Guru. While learning with a heavy heart, Allauddin handed over the entire hidden earnings to his guru. The grandmother as well as the Ustad were bewildered at his honesty and samaritan gesture. They were too astunded to utter another word, but allowed Allauddin to part with their blessings.

2.2 Life at Rampur

Rampur was then the most important seat of Hindustani Classical music with almost five hundred famous Court musicians who adorned the Rampur Nawab's Place. They were exponents of Dhrupad, Dhammar, Khayal, Tappa and Thumri as well as some of the greatest Kathak dancers. There were some of the top instrumentalists who were proficient in Been, Sursringar, Rabab, Surbahar, Sitar, Sarangi, Shenai Flute, Pakhawaj, Tabla and various other instruments. All these musicians basked in Ustad Wazir Khan's glory. They centred around him, as he was the nayak gayak (main leading singar) and principal Court Guru.

It was almost six months before Allauddin could meet Ustad Wazir Khan. The sentries (guards) never allowed him to enter his mansion. He became so desperate that he decided that he will commit suicide. And as a last resort bought four tolas of opium in case he failed to meet the Ustad.

One fine evening. His Highness Nawab Hamid Ali Khan Bahadur, the Ruler of Rampur, was on his way to attend the theatre. He often frequented musical plays and dramas which he wrote himself and these were set to music by his Guru Wazir Khan. Allauddin used this opportunity and prostrated himself before the Nawab's horse-driver carriage, which stopped just before him. The guards immediately gathered around him to clear off the road, the on lookers huddled and soon there was a commotion. They were about to beat him, when the Nawab intervened having been distracted to the noise caused by this incident. Allauddin carried a letter written in Urdu from a Maulavi. It suggested that Allauddin wanted to learn music desperately and due to failure in meeting Ustad Wazir Khan he was determined to commit suicide and thus none should be held responsible for this act. The letter was shown to the Nawab. After going through it, the Nawab asked his guards to search him further and recovered opium.

The Nawab was simply perplexed to know the reason of such a desperate step. He could not believe that anybody having such a passion for music wanted to take such a drastic measure because he was unable to meet his chosen Guru. He asked his men to return to his palace and did not visit the theatre that evening. The Nawab was not only a great patron of music and culture but also a great connoisseur, a versatile musician and litterateur. He put Allauddin to various tests and trials. First, he enquired of him as to how much he knew about music. Allauddin told him about the instruments that he could play, mainly the Sarod. Hearing that, the Nawab had his attendant brought in all the Indian and Western instruments ! He had about fifty varieties. Young Allauddin played them all expertly. The Nawab was truly amazed. Then he asked him " What else do you know ?" Flat came the answer "I can notate anything and everything that I hear". Nawab said : "Is that so ? Can you notate what I will sing ? "Yes", was the confident answer. Hamid Ali Khan was not a great singer but he knew throughly different styles of singing and started singing short pieces.

Allauddin who was given paper and pencil had already started notating and sang back the pieces. By then, the Nawab was really wonder - struck finding such as marvel of talent and at the same time a little annoyed, too, seeing the pluck of the young man. So he started singing some

'Gamak Taans' hoping to put the boy off. Allauddin could notate that too. By then he realised the Nawab's annoyance on seeing his red flushed face. So he acted immediately by showing his extreme humility and said, with folded hands: "No Hazoor I cannot do Notation of this. You made it too difficult for me." That pleased the Nawab immensely. He said : "Yes, yes, you need more Taalim but actually you are quite good as you know." Saying this, he called his attendant and told him to call Ustad Wazir Khan immediately. All arrangements were made for the grand *"Ganda"* ceremony which was followed with trays filled with gold coins, sweets and cloth materials according to the custom which are supposed to be given by disciple to the Guru. Thus Ustad Wazir Khan tied the *Ganda* on the right hand of Allauddin. The Nawab also arranged some sort of financial prop for Allauddin's sustenance by asking him to play the violin for the Rampur Band, for which he could get twenty five rupees each month. The Rampur Band consisted of a group of seventy musicians with all time greats of their class and styles. Allauddin had rented a large room above the ground floor of a building. After spending the whole day at the Music Club where they also rehearsed the band some of the eminent musicians, such as, Enayet Hussain, Saswanwale, Haider Khan, Raza Hussain, the Vocalists, Mohammad Hussain, the Beenkar, Nasir Ahmed, the Surbahar, Sitar, Fida Hussain, the Sarodist used to stop over - Allauddin had a huge pot of tea brewing ready for them.They used to spend a couple of hours with him. After gossiping they would start talking of other musicians mostly criticizing their way of singing or imitating them which ignite their egoes and would start showing off by singing rare *'Bandishes'* of their own Gharanas. This was a windfall of Allauddin and through many years this went on specially during the first two and a half years, after his becoming the disciple of Wazir Khan and when he was not given any time or opportunity by his Guru to learn. He learnt thousands of rare Dhrupad,

Dhammar, Khayal, Tappa, Tarana and Gat compositions from great musicians, whom he always acknowledged as his Gurus, contrary to the most musicians one finds today who, in spite of learning or copying other masters, never acknowledged it and instead attributed that to their father and Gharana only !

It was during this period that the family came to know of his being in Rampur and again prevailed upon him and found to his utter frustration that they had arranged a second marriage for him. This time it was with a paragon of beauty, for they thought that the charming bride would put and end to his zeal and passion for music and would bewitch him to stay at home permanently. But to their utter dispair, this effort also failed to prevent him from playing the fugitive. Allauddin could not resist his wanderings in persuit of learning more and left the house for Rampur. Consequently, the whole frustration of their failure to check Allauddin fell on the innocent bride. She was pained by their affront and remarks insulting that her beauty had no worth at all if it could not charm the spouse. This was too much for the young bride to endure, so she made an abortive attempt to commit suicide. A telegram was then sent to Allauddin care of Ustad Wazir Khan narrating the incident. For the first time Wazir Khan was forced to think about Allauddin's antecedents. What was all about this ? He asked Allauddin while handing him the telegram. Casual and detached as he was, he described the incidents of his two marriages. Ustad was taken aback on hearing the tale, though that he was a crazy man for having forsaken all the wordly pursuits for his love of music. He felt guilty and repentant having neglected this young man all these years and said "I promise to teach you like my own son henceforth. But for God's sake do go to your home first and set the things right there and then come."

This paved the way for his formal training from Ustad Wazir Khan after having mastered the basics earlier. It may read like a fairly tale, seemingly unbelievable but true. His quest for music brought Allauddin to Rampur from an unknown place of East Bengal and after years of rigorous training and practice his Guru advised him to go out into the world and spread music to the deserving students . Thus after about a year or two in his hometown and in Calcutta Allauddin was offered a job by Shyamlal Khatri, a *Raees* (aristocrat) and harmonium player of repute from Calcutta in a small native state known as Maihar in Madhya Pradesh. A small town, it was surrounded by Vindhya mountain range. Baba become a great devotee of Goddess Sharada [Fig. 2.5] when he came to Maihar and went regularly to pay his respect and have *darshan* by climbing the five hundred steep steps daily. Brij Narain Singhji the Maharaja of Maihar [Fig. 2.6], who was friendly with Shyamlal Khatri wanted him to search for a versatile musician who could teach him vocal music and different instruments. Thus Allauddin Khan became the Raj-Guru and the principal Court Musician of Maihar and stayed there till his last breath. [Figs. 2.7, 2.8, 2.9, 2.10, 2.11, & 2.12]

His remuneration was quite small compared with other Court Musicians of his status in larger native States such as Baroda, Gwalior, Indore and Mysore. Though he was invited for such as job in some of these larger states later on, he did not want to leave this little place that he liked with its "Maa Sharada" and the Maharaja who gave him love and respect deserved by a Guru."(Ghosh, A. 1990)[1].

2.3 Disciples of the Gharana

Some of the main disciples of this Gharana are discussed below :

2.3.1 Ustad Ali Akbar Khan

Considered as "National Living Treasure" in India, Ustad Ali Akbar Khan is admired by both Eastern and Western musicians for his brilliant compositions and his mastery of the sarode. Concert violinist Yehudi Menuhin

Fig. 2.5. Idol of Shri Sharada Mayi - one of the manifestations of Goddess Saraswati in Maihar, Madhya Pradesh. The image is in a temple at the top of a hill near Acharya Alauddin Khan Sahibs home.

Fig. 2.6. The Maihar Palace - home of Maharaja of Maihar.

Source: Ruckert, G. (1991): Fig. 2.5
Courtesy: Smt. Usha Majumdar (2003) : Fig. 2.6

Fig. 2.7. Madina Bhavan - Baba Allauddin Khan Sahib's home at Maihar.

Fig. 2.8. Three generations - Baba with his son Ustad Ali Akbar Khan & grandson Aashish Khan.

Courtesy: Smt. Usha Majumdar (2003) : Fig. 2.7
Source: Ruckert, G. (1991) : Fig. 2.8

Fig. 2.9. Acharya Baba Allauddin Khan Sahib's room in Madina Bhavan - Ustad Aashish Khan, Baba's grandson tuning a Sursringar.

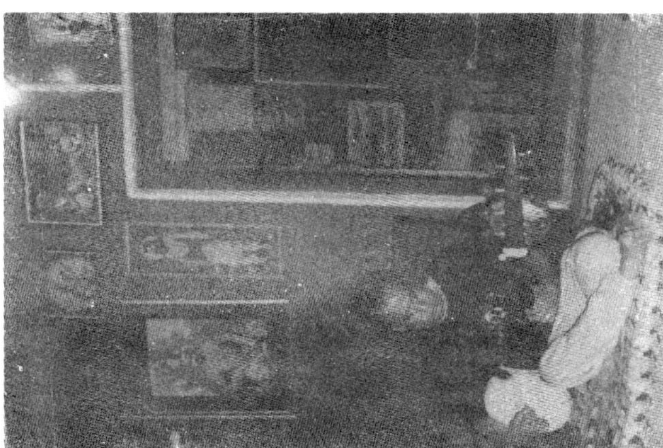

Fig. 2.10. Ustad Aashish Khan doing his riyaz in his Guru and grandfather's room, decorated with many pictures Baba was fond of.

Fig. 2.11. Every year a function is held in the memory of Acharya Baba Alauddin Khan Sahib in Maihar. Musicians of all Gharanas from all over the country perform here.

Fig. 2.12. The Samadhi of Acharya Baba Alauddin Khan Sahib in the courtyard of Madina Bhavan. It is a holy place for musicians from all over the world.

calls Ustad Ali Akbar Khan, "An absolute genius .... the greatest musician in the world," and may have considered him the "Indian Johann Sebastian Bach."

Born in 1922 in East Bengal (Bangladesh) Ustad Ali Akbar Khan (Khan Sahib) began his studies in music at the age of three. He studied vocal from his father and drums from his uncle, Fakir Aftabuddin. His father also trained him on several other instruments, but decided finally that he must concentrate on the sarod and on vocal.

For over twenty years, he trained and practiced 18 hours a day. After that, his father continued to teach Khansahib until he was over 100 years old, and left behind such a wealth of material that Khansahib feels he is still learning new things from it.

Ustad Ali Akbar Khan gave his first public performance in Allahabad at age 13. In his early twenties, he became the court musician for the Maharaja of Jodhpur. The State of Jodhpur bestowed upon him the title of "USTAD", or Master Musician. Since his father's death in 1972, Khansahib has continued his father's tradition, that of the Baba Allauddin Seni Gharana of Maihar in Central India.

At the request of Yehudi Menuhin, Ustad Ali Akbar Khan first visited the United States in 1955, and performed an unprecedented concert at the Museum of Modern Art in New York. He also made the first Western L P recording of Indian classical music, and the first television performance of Indian music, on Alistair Cooke's "Omnibus", sowing the seed for the wave of popularity Indian music in the 1960's. Since then, he has continued to tour extensively in Asia, Africa, Europe, etc.

In 1963, Khansahib was presented with the "President of India" award. He also holds the distinguished "Padma Bhusan" award from the Government of India, as well as the highest honour presented to a civilian in India, the "Padma Vibhushan" – awarded to him in 1988. Khansahib was awarded the "Kalidas Sanman" in 1991 by the Madhya Pradesh Academy of Music and Fine Arts, and an honorary Doctorate Degree in Arts from the California Institute of the Arts, in Valencia, C.A. in June of 1991, Ustad Ali Akbar Khan became the first Indian musician to be awarded the most prestigious Mac Arthur Foundation Fellowship, the "genius grant", in recognition of his excellent work in the field of creating, cultivating and transmitting the highly complex musical tradition of Northern India.

He has received four Grammy Award nominations : in 1970 for *Shree* Rag, in 1983 for *Misra Piloo*, in 1996 for then and now, and recently in 1997 for Legacy. He has also received the degree of Doctor of Literature, honoree causa, from the Rabindra Bharati University in Calcutta. He received additional awards from Dacca University, from Delhi University and form Shantiniketan (Tagore University).

In February 1997, he was the second recipient to receive the Asian Paints Shiromani Award – Hall of Fame, following Satyajit Ray. Khan Sahib founded the Ustad Ali Akbar Khan College of Music in Calcutta, India in 1956. Later he began teaching Western students in America in 1965. In 1968, he founded the Ustad Ali Akbar Khan College of Music in Marin County (California) where he continues to teach 6 classes a week for 9 months of the year.

There is also a branch of his college in Basel, Switzerland, run by his disciple Ken Zukerman, where he visits every year to teach during his yearly world tour[2].

2.3.2 Ajoy Sinha Roy

'Prof. Roy, a renowned musician, music guru and musicologist he come to be acknowledged as one of the institutional figures in the genre of Indian Classical Music, he is one of those who came in direct contact to the great maestros Ustad Allauddin Khan, his younger brother Ustad

Ayet Ali Khan as disciple. He was attached to important universities of the Country as examiner and Chairman beside having strong involvement with AIR, Doordarshan and West Bengal State Music Academy. A performer and score composer for both the screen and the stage Shri Sinha is a prolific writer of articles and treatises on music and was the editor of 'In Musica' - a Journal of the Indian Association of Music'(Roy, A. 1992)[3].

2.3.3 Annapurna Devi

Born in 1927 (Bengali 1334) during *'Chaitra Purnima'* night. Her muslim name was Roshan Ara. She was the daughter of Baba Allauddin Khan Sahib. She studied at home and learnt Bengali from a Maulavi, learnt Arabic from Ustad Ali Akbar Khan and Jahanara. She was married to Pandit Ravi Shankar at the age of 14 Years. After Pandit Ravi Shankar stayed in Maihar for 2 years, Uday Shankar visited Maihar to speak to Allauddin Khan about the marriage of Annapurna to Pandit Ravi Shankar.

After marriage, they had a son a called Subho Shankar who was born in 1942. She first performed in Maihar in front of Raja Brijnath. *Raga* performed by her was Malkauns and Baba Allauddin played the tanpura with her. At Constitution Club, she played a Duet with Pt. Ravi Shankar, Rag was*Yaman Kalyan. Later* she also performed for Jhankar, Raga was *Kausi Kanara,* 30th March 1955. In Delhi's, Constitution Club, a last days concert, duet of Sitar and Surbahar, of Pandit Ravi Shankar and Annapurna. Raga performed was *Shree*. She also had performed at the inaugral Ceremony of Ustad Ali Akbar Khan College of Music in Kolkata.

At present she is staying in Mumbai where she is still training her disciples in Music[4].

2.3.4 Pandit Ravi Shankar

Pandit Ravi Shankar was born in 1920 at Banaras in Uttar Pradesh. His father Dr. Shyam Shankar Chowdhuri was a lover of music, a Sanskrit Scholar, a Bar-at-Law and a doctorate in Political Science from Geneva. He was later employed as a professor in California University. Among his four sons the eldest was the world famous dancer Uday Shankar and the youngest is Pandit Ravi Shankar, a world famous sitar player. The other two sons Jnanendra Shankar and Rajendra Shankar were also established in their respective fields. In 1935 Pandit Ravi Shankar joined his brother's '*Nrityamandali*' as a dancer. Through it he came in contact with Ustad Allauddin Khan and become his disciple.

In course of time he became a famous Sitarist. In 1945 he was appointed music director of the *"Nrityamandali"* and also of the National Theatre. In 1949 he joined the All India Radio, where he composed several pieces of orchestra music. It was he, who introduced the '*Akhil Bharatiya Karyakram*.' He also directed the music in a number of films. He was the first Indian Musician to be invited by a film Company to direct music for a film. The film 'Charli Tales' was awarded a prize at the Venice Film Festival. In 1956 he left the AIR and went abroad to propagate Indian Music. There he was greatly assisted by Yehudi Menuhin a great Violinist of America. He became famous overnight in the western world particularly in America. After George Harrison, the great Beatle musician became his disciple, people started looking upon him as a deity. He founded the Kinnar School of Indian Music in USA. His book my music my life is a notable work. He has numerous gramophone records and C.D.'s to his credit both solo and duet (with Ustad Ali Akbar Khan and Yehudi Menuhin). He has been honoured with several awards and titles including the Sangit Natak Academy Award, Padmashri, Padma Bhushan in late 60's and Padma Bibhushan in 1982; the spirit of India Award in 1990; Japan's Fuknoka Asian Cultural Grand Prize of 1990. He was made a Member of the Rajya Sabha of India in 1986. Recently the Maestro was conferred the title Bharat Ratna[5].

2.3.5 Nikhil Banerjee

'Born in 1931 in a musically endowed family, Nikhil Banerjee was a gifted child prodigy who had the benefit of an early initiation in the art of Sitar playing from his father Jitendra Nath Banerjee. He astounded the music world when he bagged the First Prize in the All Bengal Sitar Competition at the tender age of 9 years. His achievement won him the patronage of the Maharaja of Gouripur who arranged for tutelage with the maestro Pandit Birendra Kishore Roychowdhury. He honed Nikhil's in born talents and then recognizing that this lad was destined to become the all time greats, sent Nikhil to Baba Allauddin Khan, the patriarch of the Maihar Gharana. In the hands of Baba Allauddin Khan the genius of Nikhil Banerjee found full flower in 6 years of relentless riyaz (practice). Between 1952 and 1956, Nikhil came under the creative spell of Ustad Ali Akbar Khan the sarode maestro who in turn was destined to play a crucial role in the performing carrier of Nikhil Banerjee. He eventually joined the Ustad Ali Akbar Khan College of Music and continued to serve in both Calcutta and California to his last days. It is but natural that there were extensive demands on the talent of an artiste so gifted. Nikhil Banerjee thus had the distinction of being associated with the Rabindra Bharati Unviersity as well as the Viswa Bharati University. He was also the visiting professor of Music at the American Society of Eastern Arts (AESA)'.[6]

'During his last years Nikhil Banerjee came under the creative spell of Smt. Annapurna Devi, the exceptionally gifted daughter of Acharya Baba Allauddin Khan. She transmuted his natural gifts like a catalyst that gave him the golden touch. During the whole period of growth and development Nikhil Banerjee tempered the austerity of Baba Allauddin Khan, the depth of Ustad Ali Akbar Khan and the essence of Annapurna Devi's classicism with the lyrical touch of Amir Khan's *gayaki* (singing) style interpolated in his interpretation. Although a shy introvert at heart, he became an extrovert when he expressed himself with his beloved sitar. The Government of India conferred upon him Padmashri during his lifetime and the Sangeet Natak Academi honoured him in 1974. He was awarded Padma Bhushan posthumously in recognition of his greatness. Nikhil Banerjee passed away on January 27, 1986 at the age of 54 leaving behind a rich legacy of his music and a fragrant memory that lingers on'[7].

2.3.6 Timir Baran Bhattacharjee

Timir Baran Bhattacharjee was born at Calcutta. He had his training in playing sarode under Radhika Prosad Goswami and Ustad Amir Khan. He was then 14-15 years old. When he was 20, he had the opportunity in listening to Ustad Allauddin Khan's sarode recital. He became very much attracted to Ustadji and wanted to be his disciple. Ustadji asked him to play on sarode and he became fascinated by his brilliant performance. Timir had to obtain permission from Amir Khan as desired by Ustadji. He then went to Maihar and received further training from Ustad Allauddin Khan and became his most favorite disciple. In 1930 he got acquainted with Uday Shankar and joined his dance troupe as a conductor of background orchestral music. He earned all round approbation in Europe and America for his accompanying orchestral music which greatly heightened Uday's dance performance. In 1934 he left Uday Shankar troupe. But at the request of Uday Shankar, Timir Baran persuaded Ustad Allauddin Khan to go in Uday Shankars dance troupe as the music collaborator. After a lot of hesitation Ustadji ultimately agreed and accompanied Uday Sankar troupe to foreign lands. For some time Timir Baran joined Madhu Boses drama dance troupe, 'Calcutta Art Players' and produced and directed the background music for stage plays Alibaba, Bidyotparna, etc. His orchestra accompanying the dances of Sadhana Bose on stage was highly acclaimed by the enthralled Calcutta audience. He was reckoned almost as an wizard of Sarode and instrumental orchestra. Then he joined new theatres at Calcutta as the music director and directed the music of several films including *Bijoya, Devdas* (Hindi version) *Pujarin* (Hindi), *Adhikar*. He was also a good vocalist and could play several musical instruments. He cut many Gramophone records/Discs containing his solo performance (Sarod) as well as orchestral music innovated and conducted by him. He passed away on March 29, 1987 (Bhattacharya, T. 2004)[8].

2.3.7 Pannalal Ghosh

Pannalal Ghosh was born in 1911 in Barisal (East Bengal). His father Aksaya Kumar Ghosh was a good sitar player. He used to hear him play every day and this developed a taste for classical music at an early age.

He went on improving in the art of flute-playing and in 1934, when he was 23 years old, he was booked for giving tunes in a film company in Calcutta.

While working in the films he came in contact with Master Khusi Muhammad who was an excellent harmonium player in 1937. In 1938, he went on an European tour Sarai Nritya Kala Mandali as its Music Director. On return from his tour he learned that Master Khusi Muhammad had passed away. So in 1939, he started learning music from Girija Sankar Chakravarti.

In 1940 he went to Bombay and worked there as Music Director in some of the film companies. Owing to heavy work in films he could not find much time in practicing at home. So he left the films. In 1947, he started learning music from Ustad Allauddin Khan. He made rapid progress under his training.

He was invited to many music conferences and was ultimately appointed Director of *Vadya Vrinda* (Ensemble of Instruments) in A.I.R., Delhi. He was an excellent composer and conductor. He composed many tunes for A.I.R., of which the most famous is that of Vande Mataram.

He taught his art to his son-in-law Devendra Murdesvara who has earned good reputation as flute player.

He passed away on April 20, 1960, when he was only 49 years old. (Singh, T.J. 1995)[9].

2.3.8 Bahadur Khan

A well known sarode maestro, was born in Brahmanbaria (now in Bangladesh). In his boyhood he was taken to Maihar by his uncle Baba Allauddin Khan and given an intensive and rigid training under his care. He became a top-ranking instrumentalist in radio, television and in music conferences in India and abroad. He visited several countries of Europe as a performing artist and was the music director of a number of films. His compositions and direction for 'Pancha tantra' and other productions for the 'Little Ballet Troup' set a new trend in music for the stage. He expired on 3rd October 1989 (Das Sharma, A. 1993)[10].

2.3.9 Sharan Rani Mathur

Born in 1929 at Delhi, Sharan Rani has come to the front rank on sheet merit. Contrary to orthodox ideas, she took to music in her childhood and had to work her way up under heavy odds and facing great objection. The foundation of her brilliant musicianship was laid by the greatest ever known Sarode maestro Ustad Allauddin Khan and nurtured by her illustrious son Ustad Ali Akbar Khan. The disciplined and rigorous training under these stalwarts has wielded the strongest influence on the technique of Sharan Rani's Sarode playing. She has developed the virtue of perfectionism in her performance while retaining the individuality of expression. She is an M.A. of the Delhi University. She has travelled extensively giving concerts in Asia, Europe, Australia, Fiji Islands and America where her music is adorned in thousands of homes. She was honored with many titled and awards like 'Sahitya Kala Parishad', Tandravilas Acharya, the Padma Shri and Sangeet Natak Akademi Award[11].

2.3.10 Hariprasad Chaurasia

Pt. Hariprasad Chaurasia hails from Allahabad in Uttar Pradesh. He was born in 1937. He started learning the elements of classical vocal music from Pandit Raja Ram, a vocalist from Allahabad. Within a year of his training in vocal music, he had a chance to hear a flute recital by Pandit Bholanath, a noted instrumentalist from Benaras. He later decided to learn under his guidance, this was followed much later by period of further training under Shrimati Annapurna Devi, the talented daughter of Padma Vibhushan Allauddin Khan Saheb. Hariji first performed outside India at the prestigious Shiraz Festival in Iran (Source: Cassettee by Navras Records Ltd.)[12].

2.3.11 Sisir Kona Dhar Chowdhury

Born in 1939 at Shillong to Dr. B. Dey. She was initially trained in violin under the guidance of Moti Mitra. Later she had received talim from Pandit V.G. Jog. In a very short time she became renowned all over India. She later became a disciple of Ustad Ali Akbar Khan.

In 1954, she got the first prize in the Tansen music competition. She represented India at Nepal in 1970 on the Festival of Independence at Nepal. She was a professor at the Rabindra Bharati University[13].

2.3.12 Indranil Bhattacharjee

Born in 1942, he is the son of Timir Baran Bhattacharjee, a distinguised player who himself happened to be the disciple of Ustad Allauddin Khan. Indranil was trained by both his father as well as from Ustad Allauddin Khan. He was a senior faculty member at Rabindranath Tagore's Visva Bharati University in Shantiniketan, West Bengal. He expired at the age of 61.[14]

2.3.13 Aashish Khan

Aashish Khan was initiated into North Indian Classical music at the age of five by his grandfather the legendary Acharya Baba Allauddin Khan Sahib, exponent of the "Senia Beenkar" and Senia Rababiya Gharana founded in the sixteenth century by Mian Tansen the court musician to Emperor Akbar. He learnt from his father Ustad Ali Akbar Khan aunt. Smt. Annapruna Devi, presently the leading exponts of the "Senia Gharana" in the Beenkar and Rababiya anga of the Dhruvapada style.

Aashish Khan gave his first public performance at the age of thirteen with his grandfather on the National Program, New Delhi, and in the same he performed with his father and grandfather at the "Tansen Music conference" Calcutta. Aashish Khan pioneered in the establishment of the "World music" genera, as a founder of the Indo-American group, "Shanti" in 1969-70 and later, fusion group, "The Third Eye", was first to write a Sarod Concerto in the "raga" form. With Pandit Ravi Shankar, he has worked on many musical projects for both film and stage, including Satyajit Ray's *"Apur Sangsar"*, *"Parash Pathar"* and Sir Richard Attenborough's film "Gandhi". He has also worked with Maurice Jarre on John Huston's film 'The Man who would be King, on David Lean's "A Passage to India" and composed music for Tapan Sinha's films,"Joturgriha and Aadmi our Aurat". Aashish Khan has collaborated with such diverse Western musicians as John Barham, George Harrison, Ringo Starr, Eric Clapton, Charles Llyod, John Handy, Alice Coltrane, Emil Richards, Dallas Smith, Dan Pope, Jorge Strunz, Ardeshir Farah, and the Philadelphia String Quatret. His recordings include. The Wonder Wall, Young Master of the Sarod, California Concert, Sarod and Piano Jugalbandi, Shanti, Live at the Royal Festival Hall London, Homage, Inner Voyage, Monsoon Ragas, The Sound of Mughal Court, and Jugalbandi Sarod and Sarangi Duet. In 1989, Aashish Ka was appointed to the prestigious post of composer and conductor for the National Orchestra ("Vadya Vrinda") of All India Radio, New Delhi, Succeeding such musical stalwarts as Pandit Ravi Shankar and Pannalal Ghosh. A teacher for many years, he was formerly on the faculties of the Ustad Ali Akbar Khan College of Music in San Rafael, California and the University of Washington, Seattle. While pursuing a busy career as a concert artist and composer, he teaches students throughout the U.S., Canada, Europe, Africa and of course India. In 1999 he established his music school, Academy of Indian Music in Chicago[15].

2.3.14 Dhyanesh Khan

Born in the legendary musical family Dhyanesh Khan inherited the traditional 'Seni gharana music from Late Acharya Allauddin Khan and Ustad Ali Akbar Khan. He received his rigorous initial training from his grandfather, father and aunt Smt. Annapurna Devi.

He had the privilege of performing with his father Ustad Ali Akbar Khan, brother Aashish Kan and late Prof. Nikhil Banerjee. He had and played "Duet" with eminent artists, to name a few, with Pandit V.G. Jog, Indranil Bhattacharjee, Monilal Nag and many others.

He has extensively toured Europe, U.S.A., Bangladesh in 1973, 1978, 1979 and again in 1983, his concert tours includes performances at Royal Albert Hall, London and Musee-Gimet, Paris. He was also participated in the Camden, Music festival in London in 1983. In November 1989, being invited by the I.C.C.R. he toured a number of countries in the Middle East.

He was associated with 'Ustad Ali Akbar Khan College of Music, Calcutta, and was also a Professor in Instrumental Music in the 'Rabindra Bharati University', Calcutta. He expired at the age of 49 years in October 1991[16].

2.3.15 Viswa Mohan Bhatt

Vishwa Mohan has mesmerized the world with his pristine pure, delicate yet fiery music. A disciple of Pandit Ravi Shankar, Vishwa Mohan has contributed a lot towards the development of Indian Music.

He has performed extensively in the U.S.S.R., Canada, Great Britain, Germany, Spain, France, Italy, Netherlands, Scotland etc. and throughout India. He was awarded the "Padmashree" in 2002. The Sangeet Natak Academy award in 1999. The Grammy Award in 1994 for his album, "A Meeting By The River". Presently he is busy performing all over the world and also teaching numerous disciples in U.S.A., Canada and in India.

2.3.16 Rajeev Taranath

Rajeev Taranath was initially trained in vocal music by his father Pandit Taranath and other eminent musicians and was a concert and radio artiste before he was just twenty. He is a disciple of Sarode Maestro Ustad Ali Akbar Khan and has also received guidance from Pandit Ravi Shankar and Smt. Annapurna Devi. Rajeev Taranath has toured extensively as a performer throughout India, Australia, Europe, Yemen and throughout the U.S.

In 1998 he received the National Award "Chowdiah" from the Government of Karnataka. He is currently faculty member in the Indian Music Department at the California Institute of Art in Los Angeles, California and divides his time between teaching and performing[17].

2.3.17 Deepak Chowdhury

Deepak Chowdhury's distinctive musical character has crystallized from the style of his celebrated Guru, Pandit Ravi Shankar. Brought up in a family rich in artistic and aesthetic heritage, Deepak took music instinctively. In 1966, just after graduation from Calcutta University, the eminent tabla player Kanai Dutta introduced him to Pandit Ravi

Shankar. The master accepted Deepak as his disciple, beginning a close relationship, which has continued to grow through years. Deepak Chowdhury has taken part in many of Pandit Ravi Shankar's concerts, including appearances at the Royal Albert Hall, the Royal Festival Hall and Moscow's famous Bolshoi Theatre, as well as all over India. He has participated in many festivals including the Edinburgh International Music Festival in 1984, and many other important festivals in U.K., U.S.A., France, Switzerland, Germany, Russia, Jordan, Kenya, Algeria etc. In 1984 he received the prestigious West Bengal Journalists Association award for the best music score for a stage production. The same year, while residing as a sitar tutor at the Indian Cultural Institute Bharatiya Vidya Bhavan in London, he composed the score for a production in association with the Theatre Taliesen Wales "A Word in Stargazer's Eyes". Deepak Chowdhury has also collaborated with Satyajit Ray on film and T.V. Scores. He has also composed for *"Maha Manab"*, a ballet by Amala Shankar. Despite his busy schedule he still devotes considerable time teaching hundreds of students from India, Europe and Japan.

Presently he is a senior teacher at the faculty of Instrumental Music at the Rabindra Bharati University, Kolkata[18].

2.3.18 Tejendra Narayan Majumdar

Born on May 17th 1961, like most other classical musicians, Tejendra started learning music at an early age, first with his grandfather Bibhuti Ranjan Majumdar and later with his father Ranjan Majumdar. Tejendra also received vocal training from Amaresh Chowdhury and rhythm training from Anil Palit.

After showing considerable talent in his early teens, Tejendra was taken under the guidance of Ustad Bahadur Khan, with whom Tejendra studied for 18 years. During the period he stood first in All India Radio Music

Competition (1981) and was awarded the President's gold medal and the Pandit D.V. Paluskar award, after the untimely demise of the Ustad, Tejendra studied under Ajay Sinha Roy, and was later accepted as a disciple by the greatest Indian instrumentalist, Ustad Ali Akbar Khan, from whom Tejendra gets his instructions today. Tejendra's repertoire combines elements from the Dhrupad, *Tantrakari* and *Gayaki* styles of music.

Tejendra has performed in most of the major concerts in India, including the Dover Lane Music Conference, Tansen music conference, Hafiz Ali Khan Memorial conference, I.T.C. Golden Greats Festival, Park Circus Music conference. Tejendra has also given many performances in U.S.A., Canada and Europe. He has got many Cassette's and C.D's in his credit. Besides his busy schedule he devotes time in teaching students in India and abroad.[19]

2.3.19 Partha Sarathi Choudhury

Born in 1960 in Calcutta, the city of endless cultural treasure, Patho Sarathi Choudhury is now one of the most promising Sarode players in India. He began learning Sarode at the tender age of 8 and later spent several years under the training of Ustad Dhyanesh Khan, son of legendary Sarode maestro Ustad Ali Akbar Khan. During this period he stood first in All India Radio Music Competition for instrumental music in 1976. For the last fourteen years he has been receiving rigorous training from the great Sitar maestro Pandit Ravi Shankar. The perfectionist maestro's strict and vigilant guidance has been moulding capabilities and musical talent into a unique blend of the highest order.

Partho Sarathi Choudhury has participated in several concerts and musical conferences both in India and abroad. Besides, he has accompanied Pandit Ravi Shankar on numerous occasions in India and abroad. His appearances at Paris, Germany, Switzerland, Holland and also the historic Royal Albert Hall, Royal Festival Hall, London. Moreover he has participated in the musical orchestra of Pandit Ravi Shankar which featured in the festival of India in the U.S.S.R. He keeps up with great care the pedigree and nuances of the Beenkar and Rababiya Gharana aligning with his Guru and his predecessors[20].

2.3.20 Reena Shrivastava

Reena Shrivastava had very naturally imbibed the art of music and thus, was introduced to Sitar playing by her illustrious father Rabi Chakraborty an exponent of the Seniya Maihar Gharana. Her introduction to the big stage first came her way when she was only 9 years old in the year 1970. Her performances earned her rare reviews not only in India but also abroad. Her extensive tour all over India and abroad has earned her fame and recognition in Europe, USA and Canada as well as in India. Reena Shrivastava has performed in almost all major Festivals in India and abroad starting from the Dover Lane Music conference to the Chester Summer Festival and Bath festival in U.K. Reena Shrivastava's unparalleled execution and style has made her stand popular amongst music lovers and critics and have excited listeners all over the world[21].

2.3.21 Dr. Rajeev Chakraborty

Rajeev Chakraborty started learning sarode at the tender age of six under the training of Shri Rabi Chakraborty a senior disciple of the Seniya Maihar Gharana. He began performing from as early as 9 years and earned his first recognition in the form of the "Junior National Scholarship" followed by the "Senior National Scholarship" in Music. The Prayag Sangeet Samity, Allahabad awarded him gold medals in both "Sangeet Prabhakar" in 1989 and "Sangeet Praveen" in 1991. His talent has been taking him across the globe to Europe, USA and Canada where he has participated in concerts and major music festivals which include the Bath Festival, Chester Summer Festival, Vienna Festival and Edinborough Festival. He has performed in almost all prestigious classical music concerts in India such as 'The Dover Lane Music Conference' Calcutta, 'Sangeet Natak Academy Festival', New Delhi, 'Thyagaraj Festival', Madras. He has been the music director for "*Sesh Thikana*", a Bengal film directed by Probhat Roy, '*Sambhavi*' a Hindi telefilm directed by Sudipto Chattapadhyay[22].

References

1. Ghosh, Anuradha (1990): Ustad Alauddin Khan - The Legend of Music, published by Govt. of India, pp. 21 - 38.
2. http://www.womeninfoline.com/culture/music/ustadaliakbarkhan.asp
3. Roy, Sinha Ajoy (1992): Musing on Music, published by Sri Adinath Bhattacharya [Director of Culture] Govt. of West Bengal, pp. 61- 66.
4. Personal communications with Haldipur Nityanand, 2002.
5. http://www.ravishankar.com
6. Personal communications with Chatterjee Debi Prasad, 2003.
7. Personal communications with Roy, Amit, 2003.
8. Bhattacharya, Timirbaran (2004): Udoy Pather Sahojatri, Ananda Publishers Pvt. Ltd.
9. Singh, Thakur Jaidev (1995): Indian Music, published by Sangeet Research Academy, Calcutta, pp. 466 - 467.
10. Das Sharma, Amal (1993): Musicians of India Past and Present, publisher Naya Prokash, pp. 229-233.
11. Personal Communications with Gupta Bhaskar, 2003.
12. Navras Records Ltd. Jugalbandi (Duet) Series, Pandit Jasraj and Pandit Hariprasad Chaurasia, Vol. 1, NRCC 0018.
13. Personal Communications with Barua, Manoj, 2003.
14. Personal Communications with Chatterjee Purbayan, 2003.
15. Personal Communications with Khan Aashish, 2003.

16. Personal Communications with Khan Sahana, 2003-2004.
17. http://www.rajeevtaranath.com.
18. Personal Communications with Chowdhury, Deepak, 2003.
19. Personal Communications with Chowdhury, Partha Sarathi, 2003.
20. Personal Communications with Majumdar, Tejendra Narayan, 2003.
21. Personal Communications with Chakraborty, Rajeev, 2003.
22. Personal Communications with Chakraborty, Rajeev, 2003.

3

Structural Patterns and Development Made on Sarod in the Seniya Maihar Gharana

"The Sarod used today by the Artists of the Seniya-Maihar Gharana is the result of the creative genius of Acharya Baba Allauddin Khan and his younger brother Ustad Ayet Ali Khan, both innovators in the field of musical instruments. They completely changed the size, shape and sound of this instrument. The ancient Sarod had a nine-inch belly (parchment). Its fingerboard was short and narrow and was of high carbon steel. The neck was very thick. The edge of the belly (parchment) was very sharp and was painful to hold for a long period of time." (Khan, A., 1993)[1].

3.1 Changes made on the Sarod

Acharya Baba Allauddin Khan Sahib and Ustad Ayet Ali Khan Sahib while attempting to change the structure of Sarod also improved its tonal quality [Fig. 3.1, 3.2]. They also increased the number of *taraf* (the sympathetic strings) from nine or eleven to fifteen strings. Having fifteen *tarafs* makes it easier to tune them according to the *Raag*, thus adding more resonance to the instrument. With the main strings, both Khan Sahib and Ayet Ali Khan Sahib added an optional bass *Pancham* (the 5th note *Paa*) for playing

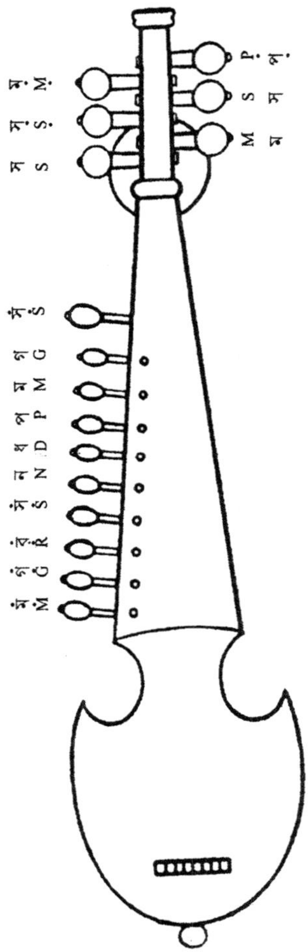

Fig. 3.1. The structure of the Sarod prior to Baba Allauddin Khan Sahib's time.

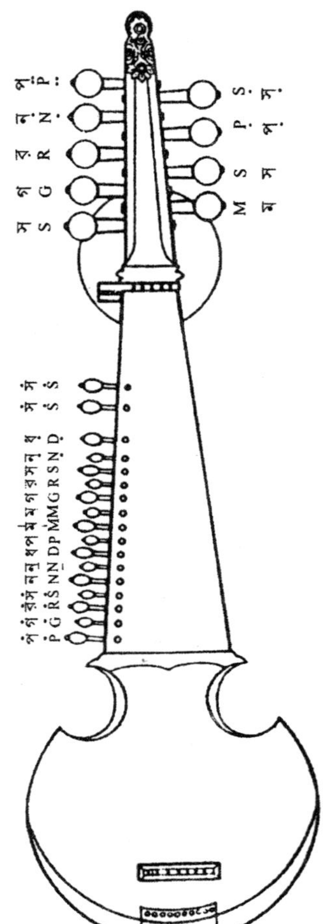

Fig. 3.2. The altered Sarod made by Ustad Ayet Ali Khan under the guidance of Baba Allauddin Khan Sahib.

Source: Khan, M.H. (1984).

Aalap in the lower register. They changed the *Ghodi* (bridge) on the parchment, which holds three layers of strings.

The top layer holds the main seven or eight strings tuned to *Maa, Saa, Paa* and bass *Saa* (bass *Paa* optional) and middle *Saa*, which supports the two *Chikari's*, both tuned into high *Saa*.

The middle layer has three opening for the three *jawari* strings to pass through.

The bottom layer has 15 openings, through which the fifteen *taraf* strings have to pass. All these strings are held by the tail piece known as *Langot*, which has been re-designed so that it will not sting the arm while holding and playing the Sarod. It also holds the strings in correct alignment, so that there is less snapping of the main strings.

They put another bridge on the neck side of the Sarod, known as *Taar-Gahan*, which means the passage for the strings. This holds the four main strings, *Maa, Saa, Paa, Saa* and the four *Jawari* strings tuned to the main note of the *Raag*. The *Jawari* strings lie on a one inch by three quarter inch flat platform. Khan Sahib added a brass *Toomba* (a hollow round shaped brass bowl) with an opening at the back of it. This gives a subtle amplification that added to the ambience. The *Toomba* is attached to the back of the neck of the Sarod, where there is a small hole drilled near the *Jawari* bridge, so that the inner overtones pass through the brass bowl - the *Toomba*. Acharya Baba Allauddin Khan Sahib changed the (*Java*) *plectrum* from metal to coconut shell. The previous Sarod maestros used to play with a flat metal wire plectrum, the same as Surshringar plectrum. This produced a very metallic overtone. Since Baba Allauddin Khan used to play the traditional Seniya Rabab (not the Kabuli Rabab) with a coconut shell *Java* (plectrum) he decided to use the same coconut shell *Java* for the Sarod. This gave a much deeper, mellower, sweeter and more melodic tone to the sound of the Sarod. This also made it possible to play *Bol* patterns and rhythmic phrases known as *Taar Paran,* a technique that was inspired by the *Bol Parans* of Pakhawaj. Acharya Baba Allauddin Khan introduced this technique. The *Java* (plectrum) plays a very important part in the technique of playing the Sarod. The right shape, thickness, size, angle and the grip made out of gauge dipped into bee's wax allows for a very firm grip on the *Java,* which was previously non-existent. Use of the right seasoned non-grained coconut makes all this possible. Shaping a good *Java* in quite tedious and time consuming. Baba's daughter-in-law Smt. Zubeda Khan learned the technique of making *Java* and she is still adept at this art of making the *Java.* The enlargement of the belly (parchment) from nine inches to eleven inches in diameter gave it a rounder and smoother looking shape and feel. This also gave a deeper and louder sound and overtone. The thinning and widening of the neck portion gave a better grip to it. This made it easier for the hand to move during fast passages, and also facilitated the playing of *Aalap, Gamak, Sapat Taan,* etc" (Khan, A. 1993)[2].

"They set the standard of thickness for the goat-skin that is pasted with glue on the belly of the Sarod parchment, not too thick or thin, more even all around for balanced overtones. He standardized the thickness of the steel plate for the finger board which created a smoother better balanced, sustained tone for *Aalap, Gamak* etc"(Khan, A. 1993)[3].

"Ustad Ayet Ali Khan presented a modified Sarod that he himself made for his nephew Ustad Ali Akbar Khan, the great Sarod maestro of today. Shri Hemen Sen of Calcutta makes most of his Sarods following meticulously the measurements and dimensions of Ustad Ayet Ali Khan's Sarod"(Khan, A.1993) [4] [Fig. 3.3].

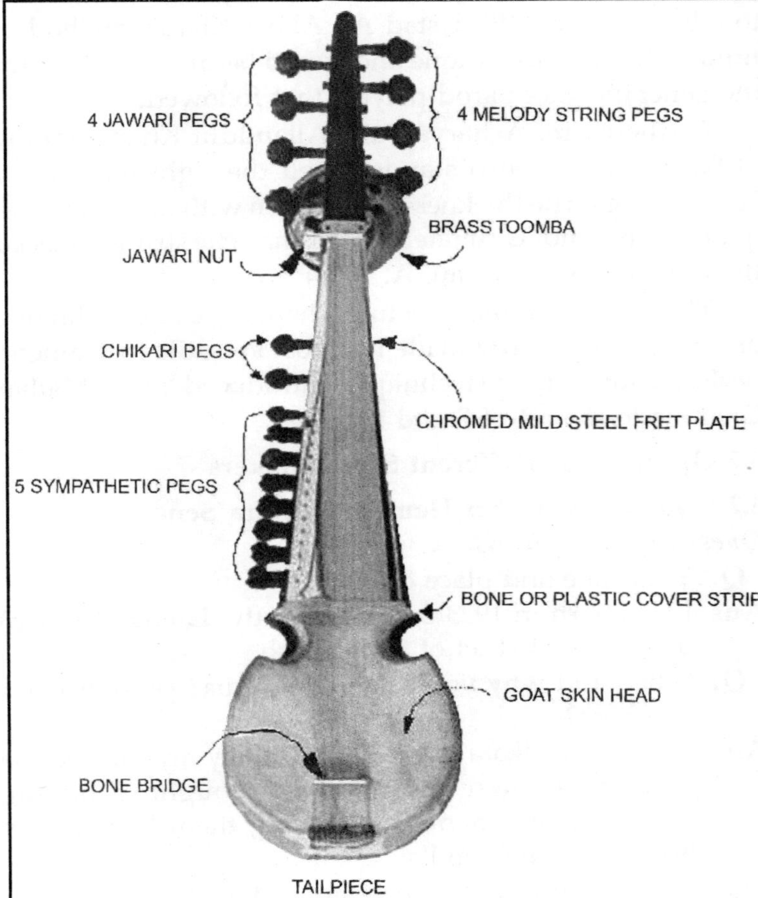

Fig. 3.3. The Structure of the Sarod played by Ustad Ali Akbar Khan. It is used by the disciples of the Senia Maihar Gharana.

Source: http://www.silverbushmusic.com/sarodeAAK.jpg

"Ustad Ali Akbar Khan made a change in the tuning of the instrument. He raised the pitch of *Saa* by tuning it to middle 'C' of piano Keyboard. Previously Sarod was tuned to a lower pitch - 'B'. Ustad Ali Akbar Khan's method of tuning, and quality of tone and sound became the ideal for the generations of Sarod players that followed.

Furthermore, Acharya Baba Allauddin Khan's family of Sarod players also standardized the right gauges for Sarod strings. The thickness was chosen with the ideal tonal qualities in mind. Ultimately the bronze *Paa* string replaced the old steel wire"(Khan, A. 1993)[5].

The changes in the structure, shape, size and technique of tuning of the Sarod made it a most versatile instrument, perfectly suited to the techniques introduced by the Maihar Gharana to the art of Sarod playing.

3.2 Opinions of Different Sarod Makers

3.2.1: Interview of Sri Hemen Chandra Sen

Questionnaire No. A1

Q. Your date and place of birth?

Ans. I was born in 1923 or 1924 (exactly date not known) in Comilla district of Bangladesh.

Q. When and why you came to Kolkata? Who brought you here?

Ans. I came to Kolkata in 1943/1944, all by myself. No one brought me here in Kolkata. I thought of buying musical instruments and selling them back at my hometown in Comilla.

Q. When and how did you start making Sarod?

Ans. I had learnt the art of Sarod making from Sri Mahendra Roy, who was a student of Ustad Ayet Ali Khan Sahib. Sri Roy also a singer and played the Sitar, besides making musical instruments. I had the opportunity to learn a great deal about Indian music and to make musical instruments from him.

Q. Who inspired you in the art of Sarod making?

Changes Made on the Sarod (as Told by Mr. Hemen Chandra Sen)

	Parts of the sarod	*Earlier*	*Modifications later*	*Who made the changes*
1.	Wood used	Teak	Tun	Allauddin Khan
2.	Drum	Longish in shape	Oval shaped	Allauddin Khan told Ayet Ali Khan
3.	Skin covering the drum	Any goat skin	Thin goat skin of good quality	Ali Akbar Khan
4.	Finger board	Steel saw plate	Stainless steel plate	Not known
5.	Jawari bridge	Elephant tusk	Deer horns	Allauddin Khan
6.	Main bridge (on the drum)	Elephant tusk	Deer horns	Allauddin Khan
7.	Chikari bridge	Elephant tusk	Deer horns	Allauddin Khan
8.	Langoat	Iron	Brass	Allauddin Khan
9.	The no. of pegs	8+1 pegs	8 pegs	Allauddin Khan
10.	Taraf pegs	11 to 13 Pegs	15 pegs	Allauddin Khan
11.	The size of Sarod	No exact size was there	About 11.5 inches	Ali Akbar Khan
12	The strings	Steel, copper	Chromesteel, copper	Ali Akbar Khan
13.	Gauges of strings	Maa=0, Saa=0 Sa= copper	Maa = 00, Saa = 0	Ali Akbar Khan
14.	Taraf strings	00 (all strings)	0, 00 mixed	Ali Akbar Khan
15.	Java (plectrum)	Wire, coconut shell	Coconut shell	Allauddin Khan

Source : Sen, H. (2004).

Opinion Contd...

Ans. Ustad Ali Akbar Khan Sahib inspired me to be a Sarod maker. I made a Sarod for Mr. Mullik, a student of Khan Sahib and I showed the instrument to Khan Sahib. After seeing the instrument Khan Sahib told me that I could be a good Sarod maker.

Q. Who made the instrument presently played by Ustad Ali Akbar Khan?

Ans. Ustad Ayet Ali Khan Sahib made the instrument, which is presently being played by Ustad Ali Akbar Khan.

Q. Have you trained any one in making musical instruments?

Ans. I have trained many disciples. Some of them are Ratan Sen, Tapan Sen, Sukumar, Nipen, Niranjan, and Dulal Kanji etc.

3.2.2 Interview of Sri Dulal Chandra Kanji

Q. Your date and place of birth?

Ans. I was born in Phalta in 1947, P.S - Harindanga, Village-Kamalpur.

Different parts of the sarod	*Earlier*	*Modifications done later*
1. Wood used	Segun Gambar, Tun	Tun
2. Drum	Was longish in shape	About 11 inches in breath
3. Skin covering the drum	Any goat skin	Goat skin, machine processed
4. Fingerboard	Steel saw plate screwed on top	Stainless steel plate, sides folded

Contd...

Contd...

Different parts of the sarod	*Earlier*	*Modifications done later*
5. Jawari bridge	Not present	Deer horns
6. Main bridge	Elephant tusk	Deer horns
7. Chikari bridge	Elephant tusk	Deer horns
8. Langoat/panthi	Iron	Brass
9. The no. of pegs	Not known	8 pegs
10. Taraf pegs	9 or 11 pegs	15 pegs
11. The size of the Sarod	No exact size was there	Drum: 11.5 inches; Total length: 47 inches
12. Java (plectrum.	Coconut shell	Coconut-shell Makonite, Fibre sheet
13. Taraf strings	00 all strings	0,00 mixed

Q. When and why you came to Kolkata? Who brought you here?

Ans. I came to Kolkata in 1952. My distant uncle Sri Kishori Naskar had brought me to Kolkata. I came here to learn how to make musical instruments.

Q. When and how did you start making Sarod?

Ans. I learnt the art of making musical instruments from Sri Kishori Naskar for about a year. In 1953/1954, I came in contact with Sri. Hemen Sen and thereafter I learnt the art of making musical instruments under

Sri. Sen for 15 to 20 years. Presently I have my own establishment called Oriental Musikraft, which supplies musical instruments.

Q. Have you trained any one in making of musical instruments?

Ans. I am still training my sons Naba Kumar Kanji and Asok Kumar Kanji.

Questionnaire No. A2

CHANGES MADE ON THE SAROD (AS TOLD BY SRI DULAL CHANDRA KANJI)

Source: Kanji, D. (2004).

Audio CD of the above interviews has been enclosed (Enclosure 1).

References

1. Khan, Aashish Ustad (1993): 'The Contribution of Maihar Gharana to the Evolution and Technique of Sarod' 'Souvenir published by Deba Prasad Banerjee.
2. Khan, Aashish Ustad (1993): 'The Contribution of Maihar Gharana to the Evolution and Technique of Sarod' Souvenir published by Deba Prasad Banerjee.
3 Khan, Aashish Ustad (1993): 'The Contribution of Maihar Gharana to the Evolution and Technique of Sarod' Souvenir published by Deba Prasad Banerjee.
4. Khan, Aashish Ustad (1993): 'The Contribution of Maihar Gharana to the Evolution and Technique of Sarod' Souvenir published by Deba Prasad Banerjee.
5. Khan, Aashish Ustad (1993): 'The Contribution of Maihar Gharana to the Evolution and Technique of Sarod' Souvenir published by Deba Prasad Banerjee.

4

Technique of the Sarod

4.1 Strings

Strings are an essential aspect of any stringed instrument, we come to know that the ancient 'Sarod' had gut strings and were tuned to lower scale unlike the modern Sarod. Wires used in today's Sarod are of different qualities and available in the market. Markets in Kolkata especially at Bowbazaar and Lalbazaar area sell Sarod strings of quite a good quality and are used by both professional and armature musicians. The Piano Treble wires by The Schaff Piano Supply Co. at Lake Zurich, also make quality strings which are used by many musicians for the Sarod instrument. These strings are known as the 'Cryogenic Steel Wires' and are available in ounces. These wires are

STRINGS	GAUGES
MAA [MADHYAM]	00 [DOUBLE ZERO]
SAA [SADJA]	0 [SINGLE ZERO]
PAA [BASS PANCHAM]	30 [BRONZE WIRE]
SAA [BASS SADJA]	26 [COPPER WIRE]
CHIKARI STRINGS	00 [EACH STRING]
JAWARI STRING	0 [ALL FOUR STRING]
TARAF STRINGS	1st, 2nd, 3rd = No.1
REST 9 STRINGS	0 [SINGLE ZERO]
LAST 3 STRINGS	00 [DOUBLE ZERO]

chemically processed in temperatures and they are of excellent quality and they hardly snap.

A chart of different gauges of strings used by musicians of the Seniya Maihar Gharana.

4.2 Fixing of the Strings on the Sarod

On the drum there is a bridge, which is tied at both ends with the help of strong strings called as the *dor* to the *langoat or panthi. [A* metal plate fixed on the belly of the Sarod]. This bridge is made of deer horns or ivory and stands upright on the drum with the pressure of all strings passing over and through it.

Generally, on the Sarod the *taraf* strings [resonators] are fixed first on the instrument. These strings are fixed to the *langoat* in a systematic method. The other end of the strings is pulled outside the body of the instrument with the help of a *sonna* [a metal implement of 5 or 6 inches in length bent or twisted at one end]. The strings are later fixed to the pegs of the *tarafs.* Above the resonators [taraf strings] we find three holes for the *jawari* strings to pass through. The strings are of '0' single zero each in thickness. The strings are fixed on one side to the *langoat* and on the other side to the pegs of the instrument. The topmost layer has two *chikari* strings [thickness 00 double zero each string], one *taraf* string ['0' single zero in thickness], and the four main strings of maa '00' double zero, saa '0' single zero, paa 30, saa 26 respectively which are fixed finally.

The strings are tied to the pegs of the instrument. A peg has a small hole, which is drilled when the pegs are made before it is used in the instrument. In this hole the strings inserted and twisted to a knot so that when the pegs are tightened the strings never slips back into its original position.

4.3 Knots

The knots are a very important aspect related to any

musical instrument. In the case of Sarod the knots helps the fixing of strings firmly to the *langoat*. The major steps for creating a good knot are as follows:

(i) Take end of the string keeping a distance of 11/2 inches from the fingers.

(ii) Cross the string in such a way so that it is created into a small loop.

(iii) Then holding the loop with the thumb and first finger is necessary of the right hand.

(iv) Winding of the loop slowly with the fixed fingers forcing the tail end to go it in the opposite direction of the left hand gives us a good knot.

4.4 The Correct Posture with the Sarod

The correct posture with the Sarod is 'half *gomukh asana.'* The instrument is placed on the lap so that the belly of the Sarod faces the person sitting with the instrument. The drum rests of the right thigh of the person with the instrument and the right hand is placed on the upper side of the body of the drum so that the instrument became perpendicular to the body and it never touches the ground.

It should be noted that the left hand is used on the fingerboard, and the weight of the instrument does not fall on the left hand. The right hand holds the plectrum or the *java*. And the left hand with a half circular grip is placed on the fingerboard with the thumb on the neck of the Sarod instrument.

4.5 The Tuning of the Sarod

The Sarod of the Seniya Maihar Gharana is tuned into natural 'C' scale. Firstly the note Saa [Sadja] is tuned. In the main string two Saa strings, *Jawari* string one Saa, two *chikari strings* tuned into higher octave Saa. Then the two Saa on the sympathetic strings. With the help of Saa all other strings are tuned. The *taraf* or the sympathetic strings are tuned according to the ascending and descending notes that are used in a *Raga*. The picture below shows the tuning of the Sarod with suddha notes with a teevra or Kari madhyam. [Fig. 4.1]

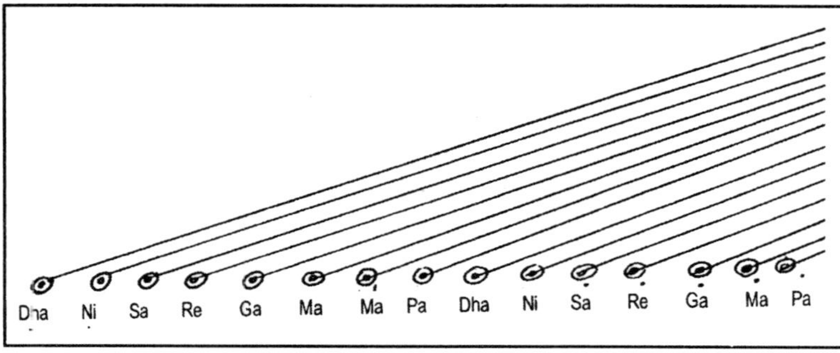

Fig. 4.1. The tuning of taraf strings. Dot below a note indicates a note of lower octave while dot above a note indicates a note of higher octave.

The main strings are tuned to maa, saa, paa, saa [from the end opposite to the taraf strings]. The *jawari* strings are tuned according to the notes used in a particular raga, but the basic tuning is Ni, re, gaa, and saa. And lastly the two *chikari* strings are tuned into *tar saptaks* saa each.

4.6 Use of the Plectrum or the *Java*

The *Java* or the plectrum used in the modern Sarod is made of coconut shell; it is in the shape of a triangle, which is slightly curved on its outer side with its one tip, pointed. Rubbing a piece of cut triangle coconut shell on a rough object makes the Java. The pieces of plectrum are then soaked in lukewarm water so that excess oil is drained out from the cut pieces.

The holding of the *Java* is tough yet artistic, the thumb should be placed on the topside with the 1st and 2nd fingers supporting it on the opposite sides. While striking the strings it should be seen that the *Java* is perpendicular in state with the strings. The rest two fingers should be resting beside the first two fingers. [Fig. 4.2]

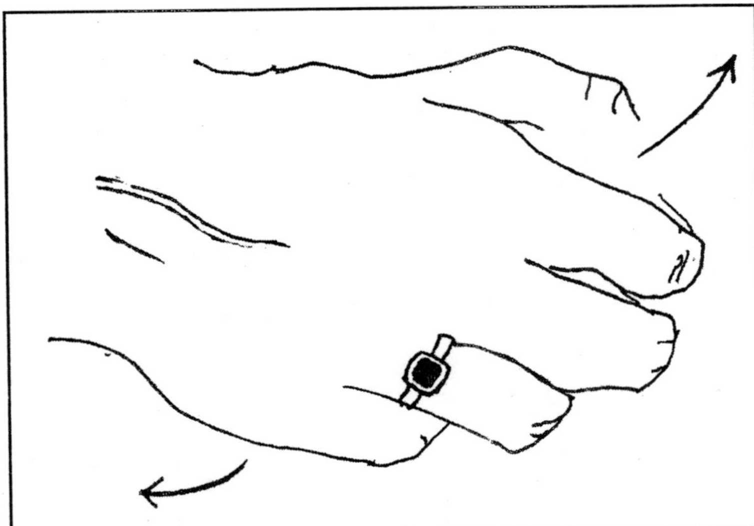

Fig. 4.2. The direction of movement of the plectrum (Java).

4.7 The Application of Fingers on the Sarod

In this topic the discussion would be about the use of the left hand on the instrument Sarod. The left hand and its fingers play a vital role in playing the instrument Sarod. The thumb and the first finger of the left hand is made into a 'V' shape for holding the instrument in a perfect grip. As the notes on the fingerboard is been played the position of the grip changes. It should be noted that the Sarod never rests on the left hand grip; otherwise it would cause disturbances in the movements of the fingers. The movement is thus flexible if the performer sits in the right posture with the Sarod i.e. half *Gomukh asana.*

The correct fingering on the correct note is given in the form of a diagram [Fig. 4.3].

FINGER [A]: This finger, which is called as the first finger for the instrument covers the following:

RE = Kharaj Suddha RE

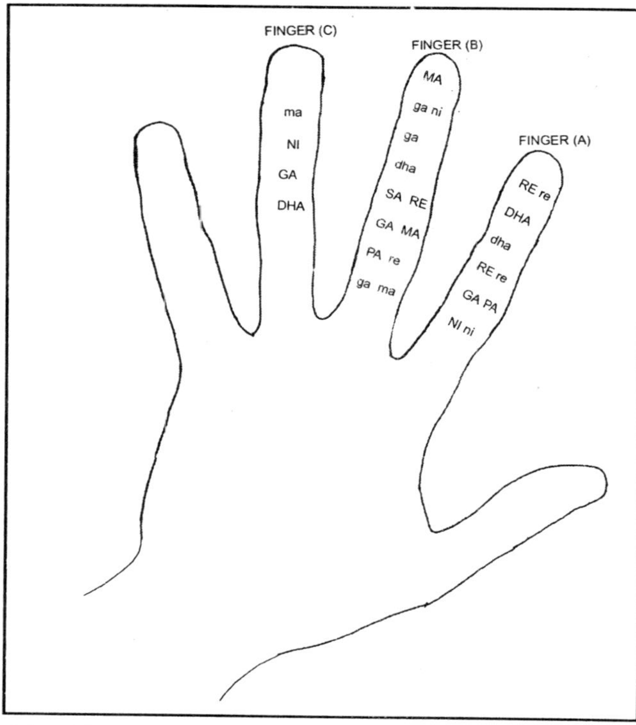

Fig. 4.3. Fingering on the Sarod : fingers to be used for corresponding notes; capital letter (eg NI) indicates suddha swaras while small letter (eg ni) indicates komal swaras.

re = Kharaj Komal re

DHA = Kharaj Suddha Dha

dha = Kharaj Komal dha

RE = Middle octave *Suddha RE*

re = Middle octave *Komal re*

GAA = Kharaj Suddha GA

PAA = Middle octave *PAA*

NI = Middle octave *NI*

FINGER [B]: This finger, which is called as the second finger for the instrument covers the following:

MAA = Kharaj Suddha Maa

gaa = *Kharaj Komal gaa*

ni = *Kharaj Komal ni*

gaa = Middle octave *Komal gaa*

dha = Middle octave *Komal dha*

SAA, RE, re, GAA, gaa, MAA, maa, PAA, DHA, dha, NI, ni SAA. All notes of the Tar *Saptak*

FINGER [C]: This finger, which is called as the third finger for the instrument covers the following:

maa = Kharaj Teevra Madhyam

NI = *Kharaj Suddha NI*

GAA = Middle Octave Suddha GAA

DHA = Middle Octave Suddha DHA

4.8 The Playing techniques with Fingering Exercises

The two basic movements on the Sarod with the plectrum of the right hand is the DA [downward movement on the strings] and the RA [upward moments on the strings] DA is denoted by the symbol '1' and RA is denoted by the symbol '– '. Further the movements can be combined to DIRI, which is the combination of DA and RA movements. In the first lesson a student is taught to play the DA, RA and DIRI on the four open strings Saa, Paa, Saa and Maa. The bol patterns like DIRI DA OR DA DIRI DA are all combinations of the basic movements DA and RA.

Some of the different *alankars,* which are practiced for different instrumentalists, are as follows:

Jhala, bol, palta, mir/meend, gamak, krintan, zamzama, etc.

Jhala: Jhala is a fast paced section of an instrumental music composition played on the Sitar or Sarod or any other stringed instruments. It is a rhythmic use of the *chikari* strings of those instruments that produces the sound of ankle bells, adding to the resonance of the main melody.

Several *laya* patterns are played on this. (Menon, R. 1995)[1]

Some of the examples are:

(A) –Da, Da, Da called *Thonk Jhala*

(B) Ra - - -

(C) Da Ra - -

(D) Da Ra – Ra

(E) – Ra Da Ra etc

Bol means a phrase of music in words or mnemonics with the rhythmic solfa syllables of *Tala* like *dha dhin dha.* In the case of the instrument *Sarod* it is the movement of the left hand with the *Java.* (Menon, R. 1995)[2]

Some examples of the Bol are listed below:

(A) Da Ra Diri Diri

(B) Diri Da Diri Da Diri Diri Da Ra

(C) Da Diri Da Ra

(D) Da Ra Diri Diri Da Ra Da Ra Da etc.

Palta are the combinations of a note in simple or complex movements. These ornaments are useful for getting the flexibility in playing music. The combinations can be with two or more notes. (Menon, R. 1995)[3].

Some examples are as follows:

(A) Sa Re Ga, Re Ga Ma, Ga Ma Pa, Ma Pa Dha…etc

(B) Sa Re Sa, Sa Re Ga Re Sa, Sa Re Ga Ma Ga Re Sa….etc

(C) Sa Ga, Re Ma, Ga Pa , Ma Dha, Pa Ni … etc

(D) Sa Re Ga Ma, Re Ga Ma Pa, Ga Ma Pa Dha, Ma Pa Dha Ni …etc

Meend is a smooth uninterrupted glide from one note to another. Its Closest Equivalent in western music is the portamento of bowed instruments (Menon, R. 1995).[4]

(A) SaReGa, ReGaMa , GaMaPa...etc.

(B) SaReGaMa, ReGaMaPa, GaMaPaDha, MaPaDhaNi...etc

References

1. Menon, Raghava R. (1995): The Penguin Dictionary of Indian Classical Music, Penguin Books India Pvt. Ltd., pp. 16 -169.
2. Menon, Raghava R. (1995): The Penguin Dictionary of Indian Classical Music, Penguin Books India Pvt. Ltd., pp. 16 -169.
3. Menon, Raghava R. (1995): The Penguin Dictionary of Indian Classical Music, Penguin Books India Pvt. Ltd., pp. 16 -169.
4. Menon, Raghava R. (1995): The Penguin Dictionary of Indian Classical Music, Penguin Books India Pvt. Ltd., pp. 16 -169.

5

The Seniya Maihar Gharana – Its Contribution towards the Field of Indian Classical Music

5.1 Acharya Baba Allauddin Khan

5.1.1 The Guru

As a preceptor Acharya Baba Allauddin Khan Sahib [Figs. 5.1, 5.2] was a hard task master and would not let his disciples go unless he was satisfied with the preparation of task by his disciples [Fig. 5.3]. Inspite of this his love and affections towards his disciples knew no bounds. Like the Guru of ancient days Khan Sahib allowed his disciples to stay with him either in his house or contiguous thereto in Maihar (a small state in Central Province now integrated with M.P.) of which he was State musician and trained them without any remuneration. He sometimes maintained such disciples who were too poor to meet their both ends. Pupils as such become his family members. The then Maharaja of Maihar was also Khan Sahib's disciple [Fig. 5.4]. But the Guru as a strict teacher did not show any special favour to the Maharaja as such. The Maharaja also realized this. He was serious as a student, meticulously followed Guru's instructions and at times stood his worth and strictures. For this his love and respect towards the Guru did not wane. Khan Sahib on the other hand was never

Fig. 5.1. Acharya Baba Allauddin Khan Sahib playing the Sarod.

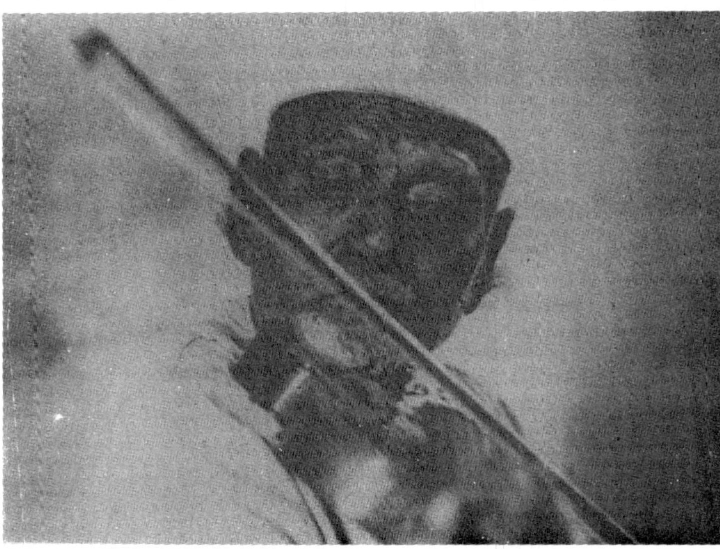

Fig. 5.2. Acharya Baba Allauddin Khan Sahib was also a virtuoso violonist.

Source: Ruckert G. (1991)

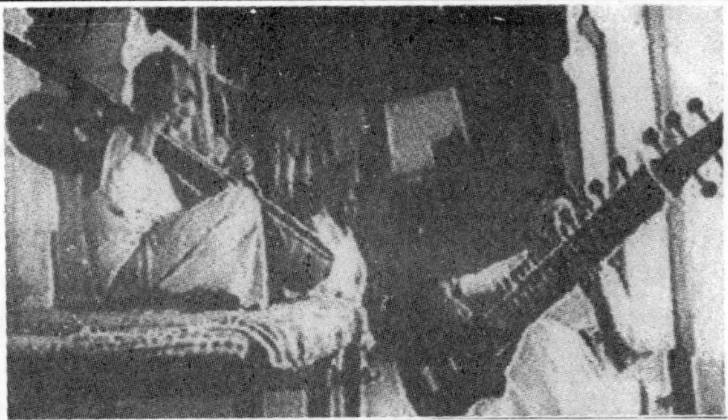

Fig. 5.3. Baba Allauddin Khan Sahib teaching his daughter Annapurna Devi.

Fig. 5.4. Baba teaching the Maharaja of Maihar, while his wife, Smt. Madina Manjari looks on.

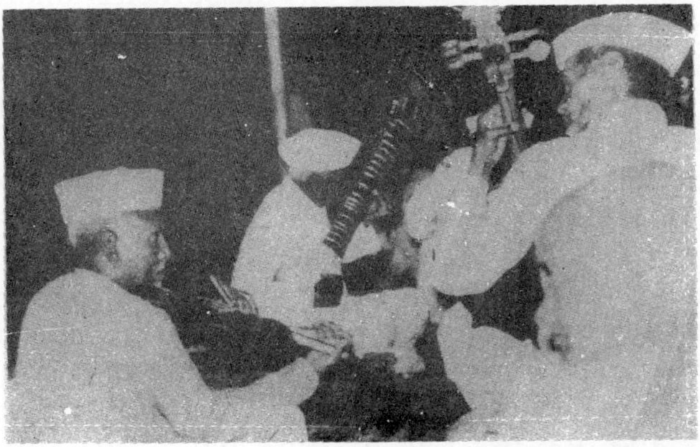

Fig. 5.5. Baba with violin conducting the Maihar Band.

Source: http://music.calarts.edu/~bansuri/annapurna.html: Fig. 5.3
Ghosh, A. (1990): Fig. 5.5

Courtesy: S. Chatterjee (2003) : Fig. 5.4

close fisted in training. He never wanted his fathomless knowledge to be kept within himself or within the members of the family.

He was always eager to teach his pupil all the treasure of the art of which he was a master. He followed the principle "The more you teach the more you become learned". Although very strict as a teacher, he always looked to the comfort of the disciples. Sometimes he would watch incognito whether the task given by him was being prepared by the disciples. If he found that the disciples were practicing and following his instructions he would be very happy and arrange on his own for the disciples' food for the day. (Ganguly, H.K. 1982)[1].

5.1.2 His Disciples

Khan Saheb's greatest contribution as a preceptor was his making of disciples. He trained and gave to he country some of the top-most instrumentalists - Ustad Ali Akbar Khan, Timir Baran Bhattacharya, Shyam Ganguly, Ustad Bahadur Khan and Smt. Saran Rani in Sarod, Annapurna Devi in Surbahar and Sitar, Pt. Ravi Shankar and Nikhil Banerjee in Sitar and Pt. Pannalal Ghosh in flute.

He also prepared a number of other artistes among whom may be mentioned Jotin Bhattacharya, Projesh Banerji, Sipra Banerji, and Suprabhat Pal in Sarod, Shyam Ganguli, Sripad Bandopadhyay, Rebati Ranjan Debnath, Mrs. Sheela Bharatram, Arun Bharatram, David, Mrs. Svarnalata Chopra in Sitar, Naidu, Roshan, Jatindra Nath Banerjee in violin, Ram Pyare and Gulgul Maharaj in Harmonium, Ghurrey Maharaj and Vinay Bharatram in Dhruvapada. He also trained a number of younger artistes like Aashish and Dhyanesh Khan, Subhendra Shankar, Indranil Bhattacharya, Robin Ghose, Sanat Banerjee, Bibek Ranjan Singh, Nirmal Kumar Roy Chowdhury, Hiren Mukherji and Basant Rai Brahmabhatt. Shri Jotin Bhattacharya, one of the pupils has given in his book 'Ustad

Allauddin Khan and his Music' and interesting description of his method of teaching.

He at first imparted sound knowledge of *Palta, meend, gamak, bol, laritan, ekahara tan, sapat tan, jhala, krintan, sparsha* etc. The students has to learn these by practising them on their instrument. Then started the practical training with *Sargam*, gat and tal, interweaving the various techniques which he had already taught.

5.1.3 The Maihar Band

Khan Saheb's another unique creation is 'Maihar String Band' consisting of 40 persons [Fig. 5.5]. Such person's ages ranged between 8 and 16 years. They were all poor illiterate unsophisticated and hailed from tribal areas. Khan Saheb took special care of them, maintained them, trained them up and made them useful citizens. Khan Saheb also invented a musical instrument from the barrel of guns declared condemned and lying in the Maharaja's armory [Fig. 5.6]. Such instruments were played in the Band. He invented new musical instruments like *Chandra Sarang, Nal Tarang* (made from Gun Barrels), Sitar Banjo [Fig. 5.7] (Ghosh, A. 1990)[2].

5.1.4 Creativity of Acharya Allauddin Khan

Some of the ragas created by Khan Sahib are Madan-Manjari (named after his wife), Mohammad, Dhavalshri, Hemant-Bhairava, Madhavagiri, Gandhi, Hem-Bihag, Bhuvaneshavri, Basanta-Behag, Chandika, Rajesri, Kaushi, Umaboti, Sarasvati, Nagarjun, Hemant, Megh-Bahar, Haimanti, Rabindra, Gandhi–Bilawal, Kedar-Manj, Subhavati, etc.

New compositions in Dhruvapada and gats of many Ragas. He combined three important roles viz. of performer, teacher, and composer. Some of his compositions are given in Jotin Bhattacharya's book 'Ustad Allauddin Khan and His Music.' (Singh, T.J. 1982)[3].

Fig. 5.6. Nal Tarang : an instrument specially devised by Baba Allauddin Khan made out of remnants of gun barrels. It is similar to the western instrument Xylophone (Jal Tarang). It was used in the Maihar Band.

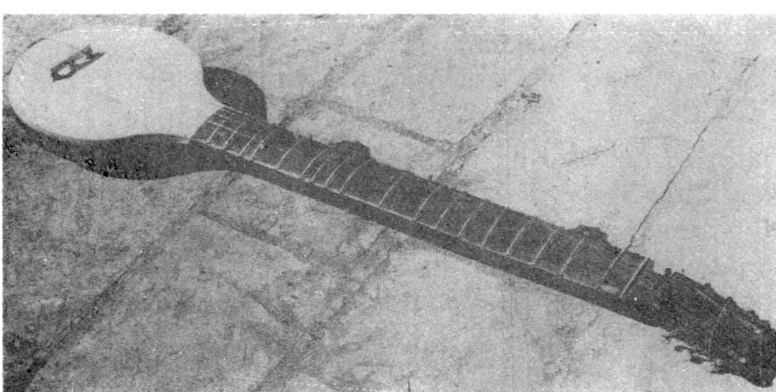

Fig. 5.7. Sitar Banjo : an instrument created by Baba Allauddin Khan by blending of two instruments - the Sitar and the Banjo. It was used in the Maihar Band.

Source: Ghosh, A. (1990).

Acharya Baba Allauddin Khan was a great maestro of the century who dedicated his whole life for music. Not only did Baba Allauddin Khan create numerous Ragas but, he also composed a few Taals, consisting of three to fourteen metricals *(Matras) like Mohan Tala (3 ½ Matras), Vijay Tala (6 Matras), Viajyananda Tala (7 Matras), Upaval Tala (8 Matras), Vikrama Tala (9 Matras), Lagukara Tala (9 Matras), Ranga Tala (11 Matras), Ranga Charam Tala (12 Matras), Ranga Royat Tala (13 Matras), Abhinandan Tala (14 Matras) etc.* (Dhar Choudhury, S. 1982)[4].

Baba Allauddin Khan Sahib's performance in his early age and that of his later age was quite different. An audio cassette released by the Megaphone Co. (Cassette No. JNLXC 1003), named 'Classicals', has a performance of the young Baba Allauddin Khan in Ragas Lalit and Jila Bilambit. From a careful study of Baba's performance, it can be conceived in his earlier days, Baba mainly stressed on Rababiya style of Baaj with short *Alaps, Laran* and *Akhara taans*. The *Bols* had different patterns and variations. Baba's scintillating recital bore testimony of his excellent *tayari*. In his later days, Baba changed his style of presentation. He used to depict Ragas with longer *Alaps* in *Dhrupad Anga,* followed by systematic *Jod* patterns and varieties of *Jhalas,* before moving on to Vilambit and Drut compositions.

5.1.5 His Multifarious Talent in Music

It is known to all that Acharya was a man of multifarious talents in music. He did not confine the specialty of Veenkar - Gharana within the instrument like Sarod, also he improvised that speciality to extend in different musical instruments. He had a mastery over two hundred musical instruments like Violin, Flutes, Xylophone, Euphonium, Saxophone etc. apart from all kinds of Indian musical instruments . He used to play on all kinds of stringed instruments by his left hand and percussion instruments on his right hand. (Dhar Choudhury, S. 1982)[5].

5.1.6 His Method of Musical Training

The system of Acharyas Musical training was really remarkable. It was an in ad seriatim process. The primary stage was the recital of tonal hymns such as :

"Paga Para Sadhu Saranam Dharey Dhyan.

Rama – Shayama – Madho Name Giridhari OM."

The tune of this hymn was, at first, practiced in vocal music and later on musical instruments. Next to it, the *Moorchhanas*, different *Paltas* and *Swara–Malikas* were taught for five years. On the second stage of training these were to be practised; the *Bols, Sapat Tans, Ladi Tanas, Jhala, Krintans, Jamjamas, Meend* and *Gamakas*. After this *Gatkari* and lastly *Alapchari* was taught. This process of training can be said, according to his version, that these divisional stages of practice (Sadhana) is the process to become merged into Param Brahma by gradual self realization.

According to the convention of Seni Gharana, there lies *Chaid*, i.e. Sadhana at first on the stage of *Alapa*; and then *Sthayee, Antara, Sanchari, Abhog* in *Vilambit laya, Vilambit – Madhya, Madhya – Tana, Druta Tanas* and the varieties of *Jhala* etc. The *Alapchari* training would be completed after learning these stages. It is already said that they always maintained the principles and conventions of Seni Gharana and of them he always gave priority to vocal music. He used to say that one, who sings well, can also play his own instruments well. The Ragas should be practiced at first vocally and then on instruments. So he taught his disciples the Tarana, the vocal style and then taught them on instrumental music. This kind of practice was prolonged for seventeen to eighteen hours a day. He often said that the practice of tone and time should be made first and then the perception of different Ragas should be taught. He uttered this truth in one of the composition in Raga Yaman.

Raga Yaman : Trital

"Gunana Ki Charcha Karie
Avagun Dur Kar Dhiraj Dhariye
Paratham Suran Tal Ko Sadhey
Raga - Bheda Guru Sey Sikhey.
Janam - Janam Bhar Sadhana Kariye
Fir Guniyan Mein Guni Kahataye"

During the discussion of Acharya's training method we, too, feel that he was not only a great creator but also a true observer. In the manner of rigid practice of the perfect pronunciation of the holy religious hymns, this sage-like-music-master used to teach his disciples methodically. All his training were always based upon the salient features of Dhrupada and Kheyal.

With the primary training of music lessons the Talas were also taught. Of course, the disciples had to learn Tabla and Pakhawaj in order to attain perfection on Talas. The *Bols* of the table had a different meaning to him, as for example.

"Na Dhin Dhin Na	=	*Baithna (to sit)*
Na Dhin Dhin Na	=	Bolna (to say)
Na Tin Tin Na	=	Karna (to do)
Na Dhin Dhin Na	=	Janna (to Know)"

Through these *Bols* Acharya wanted to say that a musician should know how to sit and demonstrate in the musical conference and after knowing this when he has realized himself, he will observe the nature of Brahma. As this blessed child of Goddess Saraswati dedicated his entire life to the cause of Indian Music so also he taught his disciples to follow his ideas. In course of his teaching he composed a few wonderful lyrics on Dhrupad, as for example:

Raga Bhairab.

"*Guru Seva Kariye Vidya Pawey*

Guru Charan Karo Pujan Tab Vidya Awey.

Guru Brahma Narayana, Guru Jnan Data

Guru Kripa Bina Vidya Nahi Pawat hai."

Acharya's own method of training was primarily based upon *Alap* and Dhrupad along with a few individual techniques. In those days the instrumental musicians followed the Dhrupad style while performing *Alap*. But the Rabab and Veen players did not follow the *Geet Alap* while playing the post - *jor* stage on their respective instruments. As for example, there are three stages of *Jor, Madh-Jor, Barabar-Ki-Jor, Gamak Jor* and *Drut-Jor*. Next to these are *Tarparan* and different parts of *Jhala* such as - *Ladi Jhala, Thok Jhala, Ulta Jhala*. Acharya introduced this *Baj* of Veenkaras to Surbhar and Sitar and also that of Rabab and Sursringar to Sarod. Previously, the Veenkaras and Rababiyas used to play the stages from *Jor* to *Jhala*. Later, the Sitar players, the Surbahar Players and the Sarod players followed it in order to maintain the tradition.

Acharya also improvised his *Ghar* and by introducing further seven sub divisions of the six previous stages of Gat i.e. *Ati Vilambit, Vilambit, Madhya Vilambit, Madhya Drut, Drut* and *Ati Drut*. Regarding this Acharya's contribution is : that he added a different style a midst *Masidkhani* Gat. Previously the *Bols* of *Masidkhani* Gat was as follows:

1 2 0 3

DIRI/ DA DIRI DARA/DA DA RA, DIRI/DA DIRI DA RA / DA DA RA etc.

These *Bols* were maintained even in course of expanding (*Vistara*) a Raga. But Acharya used to play the *Alap Anga* without a *Bol*. He was the first musician who introduced this new style in *Masid Khani* Gat. Prior to his novel invention he used to follow the tradition method like 4/4 divisions while expanding a 'Raga' . Later he introduced the new system.

Acharya often played Wazirkhani Gat a novel invention Guru Wazir Khan. The *Bols* of this Gat under medium tempo (*Madhya Laya*) are as follows : 1 2 0 3

Da Diri Da Ra / Da Diri Da Ra / Da Diri Da Ra / Da Diri Dara Dadiridara

It not only distinguishes itself from the *Masidkhani* Gat but also its variety of reaching the '*Som*' just after playing the short composition of two *Matras* is worth-notice. This specially is maintained all through.

Acharya invented a new Bol on the Sarod - playing. Previously the Bol '*Diri*' was used excessively. He was the first musician who introduced the Bols '*Dara Dara*' in place of '*Diri*'. It was an erring knowledge from his previous Guru Ustad Ahmed Khan of Rampur.

The musicians, prior to Acharya Allauddin Khan Sahib were normally adept in one particular stage of the different steps of musical demonstration. As for example, some were specialist in *Alapa,* some were experts in playing *Razakhani* or *Masidkhani* Gats and a few of them were famous for their mastery in *Layakari* or in *Jhala*. But Acharya Allauddin Khan distinguished himself from them. He learnt every step of the *Vadan Angas* accurately, gained mastery over them and also trained those of his disciples in totality. And this his descendants still have been following his path to their utmost care.

There we find in the demonstratation the totality of a Raga, its aesthetic side, a full-fledged *Alap* of the *Dhrupadiyas* varieties of the *Gats, Layakaries* and *Tanas* and the like. (Dhar Choudhury, S. 1982).[6]

5.1.7 His Contribution as a Performer

As a performer, he was quite a different artist. He was an adorer of 'Sur - Brahma' whether at home or outside.

He never split his musical personality. And for this we may notice a harmony between the sentiment and art in his music. There, one may feel an eagerness for absolute self-surrender to 'Sur-Brahma', not before the listeners. To him the opinion of True Music is as follows : To a musician, music should be the Supreme Deity, who will be worshipped with the eagerness of an undivided mind and tears shall be his ritual ingredients. Listening to that music, the listeners will be spell-bound to forget to cheer the musician, is such an ideal music. The note, which is brought forth from the core of the heart of the musician, may lose its purity amidst the mirage of musical conferences. Our music is composed by the sages and Rishis. It has originated from the "Naad Brahma." (Dhar Choudhury, S. 1982)[7].

5.2 Ustad Ali Akbar Khan

Ustad Ali Akbar Khan Sahib [Fig. 5.8] is one of today's most accomplished Indian Classical Musicians. Considered a "National Living Treasure", he is admired the world over for his brilliant compositions and his mastery of the Sarod. His contribution towards the field of Indian Classical Music is enormous and he has become a legend in his lifetime.

Fig. 5.8. Ustad Ali Akbar Khan, the Maestro, playing the Sarod in a concert in San Francisco.

Source: Ruckert, G. (1991)

5.2.1 Creation of Ragas

He created many new Ragas which have been enlisted below[8].

Chandranandan	Jogia Mallar
Gouri Manjari	Asha Maand
Lajwanti	Loam Nat
Mishra Shivranjani	Loam Nat Bilawali
Medhavi	Chhaya Tilka
Alamgiri	Maluha Chhaya
Madhumalati	Malayalam / Alam Malaya Smriti Smriti
Hindol Hem	Alam Bhairav
Pahari Jhinjhoti	Narayani Gouri
Kaushi Jogia	

5.2.2 Contribution as a Music Director

Ali Akbar Khan Sahib had worked as a music director in many films and some of them are[9]:

Films	*Director*
1. Devi	Satyajit Ray
2. Khudito Pashan	Tapan Sinha
3. Ajantrik	Ritwik Ghatak
4. Antarikha	Rajen Tarafdar
5. Andhiyan	Chetan Sharma
6. Jhinder Bondi	Tapan Sinha
7. Little Buddha	Bernardo Bertolucci

5.2.3 Creation of Taals

Ustad Ali Akbar Khan Sahib had also devised a new taal of five and a half (5 ½) beats which he has named *Sasanka*. This taal is derived from *Rupaka* of seven beats. The structure of *Rupaka* taal is as follows :

123 / 45 / 67

In the case of '*Sasanka*' taal it is played as 123½ (123 double), the last portion being in double tempo makes it, 1½ so that altogether we have 51/2 beats Ustad Ali Akbar Khan Sahib had similary devised a '*Jhampaka*' tal of 8½ beats from *Jhamptal* of 10 beats a *Saraswati* tal of 11½ beats from *Dhamar* of 14 beats. (Arup Silpa Gosthi, 1972)[10].

5.2.4 Ali Akbar College of Music (Kolkata)

Ali Akbar College of Music [Fig. 5.9] specializes in Indian classical instrumental music. The teaching entirely follows the tradition and the method introduced by Acharya Baba Allauddin Khan.

14th April (Poila Baisakh) happens to be the birthday of Ustad Ali Akbar Khan. On the same date in the year 1956 at Ballygunge 16, Mandevillae Gardens Governor of West Bengal Late Harendra Kumar Mukhopadhaya, Dr. Kalidas Nag etc. inaugurated the Ali Akbar College of Music. At the inaugural ceremony Ustad Baba Allauddin Khan Sahib's daughter Smt. Annapurna Devi played Raag *Puriya Dhyaneshree* and this was her first appearance in Kolkata with the instrument Surbahar. Later on Ustad Ali Akbar Khan Sahib played Raag *Kirwani*. This was the second institution imparting training of Baba Acharya Allauddin Khan Sahib, the first being the Acharya's residence at Maihar. (*Source* : Desh, 8th baisakh, 1363).[11]

Some of the teachers imparting training at the Ali Akbar College of Music were :

Teacher	*Subject*
Pandit Nikhil Banerjee (Late)	SITAR
Ustad Aashish Khan	SAROD
Anil Mallick	SAROD
Sisir Kana Chowdhury	VIOLIN
Sunil Chatterjee	VOCAL
Mahapurush Mishra (Late)	TABLA
Bharati Bose	SITAR
Ashutosh Ganguly	GUITAR
R.D. Khan	VOCAL

(Souvenir on Baba Allauddin Khan)[12]

Fig. 5.9. Students doing riyaz at the Ali Akbar College of Music in Kolkata ; inset : their Guru Ustad Ali Akbar Khan.

Fig. 5.10. Ustad Ali Akbar Khan teaching an instrumental class at the Ali Akbar College of Music, California.

Source: Arup Silpa Gosthi (Souvenir, 1972) : Fig. 5.9
Ruckert, G. (1991) : Fig. 5.10

5.2.5 Ali Akbar College of Music (California)

Ali Akbar College of Music (AACM) [Fig. 5.10] is the only institution outside India which teaches classical music of the Seniya Maihar Gharana founded by Late Acharya Baba Allauddin Khan Sahib . Ustad Ali Akbar Khan founded AACM in the U.S. in accordance with his father's wish to spread the unique music of North India to the rest of the world.

Ali Akbar College of Music was established at its present location in San Rafael, California in 1974. Branches of the college have also been established in Fremont, California and Basel, Switzerland. Ustad Ali Akbar Khan Sahib teaches the most of the classes himself. Tabla maestro Pandit Swapan Chaudhuri teaches percussion.

5.2.5.1 Teaching at AACM

Instruction is offered in Hindustani Classical Vocal and Instrumental Music in the Ali Akbar College of Music (AACM). Ustad Ali Akbar Khan teaches several vocal classes a week and all students are encouraged to participate.

(A) Instrumental Music : Khan Sahib also teaches three or four levels of instrumental classes weekly. Most students learn sitar, sarod or violin (there is usually a special class for bowed instruments), but one can learn on any instrument. Guitars, Cellos, Flutes and Basses are not uncommon at the Ali Akbar College.

(B) Percussion : Pandit Swapan Chaudhuri teaches tabla individually or in small groups arranged by the level of the students. Tabla students gain accompaniment experience by playing for vocal and instrumental classes and by practicing with other students[13].

5.2.6 His Worthy Disciples

SAROD	
Aashish Khan	Dhyanesh Khan (late)
Saran Rani Mathur	Rajiv Taranath
Tejendra Narayan Majumder	Shyamal Nath
Somesh Chatterjee	D.L. Kabra
Anindo Banerjee	Ken Zukerman
Bruce Hamm	David Trasoff
George Ruckert	
SITAR	
Nikhil Banerjee	Allyn Miner
James Pomeranz	Bharati Bose
Purbayan Chatterjee	
FLUTE	
G.S. Sachdev	
VIOLIN	
Sisir Kona Dhar Chowdhury	George Ruckert
GUITAR	
B.L. Kabra	
MUSIC DIRECTION	
R.D. Burman	Jaydev

(Personal Communications)[14, 15]

5.3 Pandit Ravi Shankar

One of the greatest living sitar virtuoso of the North Indian Instrumental music, the contribution of Bharat Ratna Pandit Ravi Shankar [Fig. 5.11] towards the field of Indian Classical Instrumental music is vast and beyond compare. He has not only taken his music to all parts of India but is also responsible for popularising the Sitar all over the world. He has collaborated with numerous renowned musicians across the globe and is considered as the Ambassador of

Indian Classical music. He has also performed with Ustad Ali Akbar Khan [Fig. 5.12] in many concerts.

5.3.1 Creation of Ragas

Pandit Ravi Shankar has created a number of Ragas. Some of them are[16];

Gangeshwari	Rangeshwari
Kameshwari	Bairagi
Bairagi Todi	Kaushik Todi
Tilak Shayam	Rasiya
Raj Kalyan	Ahir Lalit
Palas Kafi	Jogeshwari
Mohan Kauns	Yaman Manjh
Gunji Kanhara	Janasanmodini
Manamanjari	Mishra Gara
Pamcham Se Gara	Purvi Kalyan
Charu Kauns	Bhawani Bhairav
Sanjh Kalyan	Shailangi
Suranjani	Rajya Kalyan
Banjara	Piloo Banjara
Suvarna	

5.3.2 Contribution as a Music Director

Pandit Ravi Shankar has worked as a music director in many films and some of them are[17] :

Fig. 5.11 Pandit Ravi Shankar, the Maestro playing the Sitar.

Fig. 5.12. Two of Baba Allauddin Khan Sahib's most illustrious students : Pandit Ravi Shankar and Ustad Ali Akbar Khan

Source: http:// web.axelero.hu/andkozma/ravi1.jpg : Fig. 5.11
Ruckert, G. (1991): Fig. 5.12

Films	*Director*
1. Kabuliwala	Tapan Sinha
2. Pather Panchali	Satyajit Roy
3. Aparajito	Satyajit Roy
4. Apur Sansar	Satyajit Roy
5. Parash Pathar	Satyajit Roy
6. Strir Patra	Purnendu Patri
7. Nicha Nagar	Chetan Anand
8. Meera	Gulzar
9. Anuradha	Hrishikesh Mukherji
10. Khudito Pashan	Tapan Sinha
11. Gandhi	Sir Richard Attenborough

5.3.3 RIMPA Music Academy

RIMPA (Ravi Shankar Institute of Music and Performing Arts) is a non proft organization where students could receive training of Indian Music[18].

Founder President	Pandit Ravi Shankar
Honorary President	Sir Yehudi Menuhin
Teachers at RIMPA	Peter Szalai, Stephen James, Ivan Nyusztay and Andras Kozma

5.3.4 Contribution and Additions in the Sitar

Apart from performing in numerous concerts in India and abroad, Pandit Ravi Shankar added *Kharaj Pancham* and *Kharaj Sadaj* Strings which were bronze/copper wires, to avail the aesthetics of Dhrupad *Alap*. During the Drut portion the *Kharaj Pancham* and *Kharaj* SA Strings are hooked to a small hook fixed on the steel fret of the Sitar. In order to increase the range of meer the danda of the sitar was increased in breadth. So easily 5 pardah meends could be played thereafter. (Personal Communications with Chowdhury, D., 2003).[19]

5.3.5 The Ravi Shankar Foundation

Established in New Delhi this foundation will serve as a resource centre for researching Indian Classical Music and archiving the works of Ravi Shankar and other masters. Facilities such as a library, reading room, and art gallary will provide a forum for collaboration with other institutions for facilitating study courses, conferences, seminars, lectures and research in arts. The establishment will also be a venue for informal and intimate Indian Music performances and art exhibitions. The students will be introduced to the age old traditions of the *Gurukul* System of learning, where they will live, practice and breathe in the aura of music under the guidance of the *Guru.*[20]

5.3.6 Disciples of Pandit Ravi Shankar

Some of Pandit Ravi Shankar's disciples are as follows[21]:

SITAR	
Amiyo Babu	Joya Biswas
Shyamadas Chakraborty	Kartik Seshadri
Deepak Chowdhury	Kartik Kumar
Subhendra Rao	Subho Shankar
Uma Shankar	Arun Bharatram
Shamim Ahmed	Gaurav Mazumdar
M. Janardhan	Sudha Giri
SAROD	
Aashish Khan	Partho Sarathy
Aditya Verma	

Contd...

Contd...

FLUTE	
Vijay Raghav Rao	Ronu Majumdar
SHEHNAI	
Daya Shankar	
VIOLIN	
Satyadev Pawar	
OTHERS	
Viswa Mohan Bhatt	(Mohan Veena)
Gopal Krishna	(Vichitra Veena)
Barun Kumar Pal	(Hansa Veena)
Vinay Bharat Ram	(Vocal)

5.4 Smt. Annapurna Devi

Smt. Annapurna Devi, daughter of Baba Allauddin Khan had obtained *talim* from Baba and is herself a celebrated sitar maestro [Fig. 5.13]. She has performed in many concerts [Fig. 5.14] and at present is training many disciples to keep alive the tradition of the Gharana[22, 23].

5.4.1 Her worthy disciples

SITAR	
Subho Shankar	Smt. Ameena Perera
Amit Roy	Sudir Phadke
Nikhil Banerjee (late)	Gayatri Sanyal (Chakraborty)
Indira Chowdhury	Bijoya Banerjee
Anando Gopal Mukherjee	Aparna Ganguly
Namita Ghosh	Rooshikumar Pandya
Mrs. Sandhya Apte	Smt. Saswati Ghosh Guha
Dr. Hemant Desai	Smt. Prabha Agarwal
Rahamohan Das	Anant Ram
Smt. Mina Sukhatankar	Mrs. Vaze
Mrs. Sardesi	Chandrakant Sardeshmukh

Contd...

Fig. 5.13. Smt. Annapurna Devi Baba Allauddin Khan Sahib's daughter and disciple.

Fig. 5.14. Smt. Annapurna Devi and Pandit Ravi Shankar in concert.

Source : Ghosh, A. (1990) : Fig. 5.13
http://music.calarts.edu/~bansuri/annapurna.html" Fig. 5.14

Contd...

FLUTE	
Hariprasad Chowrasia	Milind Sheorey
Nityanand Haldipur (Basuri)	
VOCAL	
Gautam Mukherjee	
SAROD	
Aashish Khan	Suresh Vyas
Dhyanesh Khan (late)	Birendranath Banerjee
Amit Bhattacharya	Pradeep Barot
Supriyo Banerjee	Rajeev Taranath

5.4.2 Ali Akbar College of Music (Kolkata)

Smt. Annapurna Devi was also associated with the Ali Akbar College of Music in Kolkata. The Institution was established in 1956 and was situated in 97-B, Harish Mukherjee Road, in Kolkata. She was a Advisory Board Member of this Institution and was also a visiting professor of the college of Music when she was in Calcutta. (Arup Silpa Gosthi, 1972)[24].

5.5 Pandit Pannalal Ghosh

Pandit Pannalal Ghosh was legendary flutist and was one of the Senior disciples of Baba Acharya Ustad Allauddin Khan Sahib. He prepared a long, thick flute of his own on which he could display the *Alaap* of a raag in all registers. He played both in the Khayal style and in the *gata* style. He had composed many tunes for the All India Radio of which the most famous is that of Vande Matram. Shri B.B. Keskar director of (A.I.R.) awarded him the post of composer - conductor of the Indian National Orchestra and

Fig. 5.15. Pandit Pannalal Ghosh.

Fig. 5.16. Ustad Bahadur Khan.

Source: http://www.pifano.nl/Images/PannalalGhosh.jpg : Fig. 5.15
http://www.pathcom .com/~ericp/mi-bahadhur2.jpg ; Fig 5.16

Producer of A.I.R. Delhi. He created the bass bansuri and also introduced the six stringed tanpoora.

5.5.1 Ragas created by him

Deepavali	Pushpachandrika
Hansanarayani	Chandramauli
Panchavati	Nupurdhwani

5.5.2 His Disciples

Devendra Murdesvara (late)	Rashbehari Das
Gour Goswami (late)	Sharad Mahole
V.G. Karnad	Haripada Chowdhury (Late)
Suraj Narayan Purohit	Raghunath Seth
Azizur Reheman (Minto Da)	Fakir Da
Niranjan Haldipur (late)	K. D. Desai
Mr. Nachane.	

(Personal communication)[25]

5.6 Pandit Timirbaran Bhattacharya

In 1930 he joined Uday Shankar's dance troupe as a music director and visited places like Germany, Japan, Canada and Europe. In 1934 he had joined the famous New threatres and directed music for Bijoya, Devdas (Hindi version), Pujarin (Hindi), Adhikar.

Later he joined Madhu Bose's dance drama troupe 'Calcutta Art Players' and directed background music for stage plays like Alibaba, Bidyutparna etc. In 1942 he presented through the All India Radio, an Instrumental ensemble based on Rabindranath Tagores 'Khudito Pasan'. He had also visited Mumbai and Pakistan and worked as a

Fig. 5.17. Pandit Nikhil Banerjee - another distinguished disciple of Baba Allauddin Khan Sahib.

Fig. 5.18. Ustad Aashish Khan, grandson and disciple of Baba Allauddin Khan Sahib and an eminent musician.

Source: Ghosh, A. (1990): Fig. 5.17
http://www.deshvidesh.com : Fig. 5.18

music director for stage and films. He lastly had worked for 'Star Theatre'. (Bhattacharya, Timirbaran (2004)[26].

5.7 Ustad Bahadur Khan

Ustad Bahadur Khan, son of the famous musician Ustad Ayet Ali Khan was a renowned teacher, composer music director and a solo performer. He went to Maihar where he studied the sarod with his uncle Acharya Baba Allauddin Khan.

5.7.1 His Contribution as a Music Director

Ustad Bahadur Khan directed the music of Ritwik Ghatak's film *Subarna Rekha*, for which he received an award as best music director, he also directed music for *Natun Pata* for which he was also honoured. Later he directed music in *Meghe Dhaka Tara, Trisandhyay, Yekhane Dandiye, Shvet Mayur* and *Titas Ekti Nadir Nam*. He composed background music for documentaries made on Rabindranath Tagore and Jamini Roy[27].

5.7.2 His Disciples

Manoj Shankar	Kirit Khan
Ranjan Ganguly	Bidyut Khan
Dulal Roy	Tejendra Narayan Majumdar

5.8 Pandit Nikhil Banerjee

One of the best sitar players of the Seniya Maihar Gharana. Late Pt Nikhil Banerjee [Fig. 5.15] mesmerized audiences with his melodious and scintillating performances all over the world.

5.8.1 His Disciples

Partha Chatterjee	Amit Roy
Debiprasad Chatterjee	

5.8.2 Ragas created by him

Manomanjari	Purabi Kalyan
Hem Lalit.	

(Personal communications)[28]

5.9 Ustad Aashish Khan

The eldest son of Ustad Ali Akbar Khan and grandson of Acharya Baba Allauddin Khan, Ustad Aashish Khan [Fig. 5.16] is one of the most distinguised musician of Senia Beenkar and Senia Rababiya Gharanas which trace back their origin to the illustrious Mian Tansen of the Sixteenth Century.

5.9.1 His Contribution as a Composer

He had composed music for Tapan Sinha's "Jotugriha", 'Aadmi Aur Aurat'. He had worked with Maurice Jarre on John Houston's film "The Man who would be King". In David Lean's "A Passage to India". In Clint Eastwood's Breezy. He had worked in film scores which Satyajit Roy's *Apur Sangsar, Parash Pathar* and *Goopi Gayen – Bagha Bayen*. In addition to being appointed composer and conductor for Vadya Vrinda of All India Radio in 1989-90, he has composed music for ballets and film productions.

5.9.2 His Contribution as a Teacher

Ustad Aashish Khan now teaches not only in India, but in Canada, Europe and Africa. In the United States he has taught for Ravi Shankar's Kinnara School of Indian Classical Music (1968) in Los Angeles, the University of Washington Seattle (1969-70) and for his father, Usad Ali Akbar Khan at the Ali Akbar College of Music in San Rafael, California[29].

Personal Communications with Khan, Aashish, 2004.

5.9.2.1 His Disciples

Shiraz Ali Khan	Dishari Chakraborty
Amitava Majumdar	Debanjan Bhattacharya
Aditya Verma	Abir Banerjee
Prasenjit Sengupta	Ranajit Sengupta

References

1. Ganguly, Hirendra Kumar (1982): '*Contributions of Alauddin Khan to Hindustani Music*' Journal Dept. of Instrumental Music, Rabindra Bharati University, Kolkata, pp. 12 - 17.
2. Ghosh, Anuradha (1990): *Ustad Alauddin Khan - The Legend of Music*, published by Govt. of India, pp. 21 - 38.
3. Singh, Thakur Jaidev (1995): *Indian Music*, published by Sangeet Research Academy, Calcutta, pp. 466 - 467.
4. Dhar Chowdhury, Sisirkona (1982): '*Ustad Alauddin Khan: The Great Maestro*' Journal Dept. of Instrumental Music. Vol. 2, pp. 46 - 54.
5. Dhar Chowdhury, Sisirkona (1982): '*Ustad Alauddin Khan: The Great Maestro*' Journal Dept. of Instrumental Music. Vol. 2, pp. 46 - 54.
6. Dhar Chowdhury, Sisirkona (1982): '*Ustad Alauddin Khan: The Great Maestro* 'Journal Dept. of Instrumental Music. Vol. 2, pp. 46 - 54.
7. Dhar Chowdhury, Sisirkona (1982): '*Ustad Alauddin Khan: The Great Maestro*' Journal Dept. of Instrumental Music. Vol. 2, pp. 46 - 54.
8. Personal Communications with Perera, Ameena, 2003.
9. Personal Communications with Perera, Ameena, 2003.
10. Arup Silpa Gosthi (1972): *Souvenir, published on Ali Akbar Khan.*
11. 'Desh' (8th Baisakh, 1363).
12. Souvenir published on Baba Allauddin Khan.

13. http://www.aacm.org/aacm/teaching.htm
14. Personal Communications with Majumdar,Tejendra Narayan, 2002-2003.
15. Personal Communications with Shyamal Nath, 2002-2003.
16. Personal Communications with Chowdhury, Deepak, 2003.
17. Personal Communications with Chowdhury, Deepak, 2003.
18. http://web.axelero.hu/andkozma/sishya.htm
19. Personal Communications with Chowdhury, Deepak, 2003.
20. http://www.ravishankar.org/foundation-frame.html
21. Personal Communications with Chowdhury, Deepak, 2003.
22. Personal communications with Haldipur Nityanand, 2003
23. Personal communications with Banerjee Supriyo, 2003.
24. Arup Silpa Gosthi (1972): '*Souvenir, published on Ali Akbar Khan*'.
25. Personal communications with Haldipur Nityanand, 2003.
26. Bhattacharya, Timirbaran (2004): *Udoy Pather Sahojatri,* Ananda Publishers Pvt. Ltd.
27. Personal Communications with Majumdar, Tejendra Narayan, 2003.
28. Personal communications with Chatterjee Debi Prasad, 2003.
29. Personal Communications with Khan, Aashish, 2004.

6

Opinions of Musicians About the Contribution of the Seniya Maihar Gharana

Senia Maihar Gharana is considered to be one of the foremost in the world of Indian Classical Music today. All musicians and musicologists hold Acharya Baba Allauddin Khan Sahib, the father of this Gharana, in high esteem. He devoted his entire life towards the development of Indian Classical Music and has given to the world Maestros such as Ustad Ali Akbar Khan, Pandit Ravi Shankar, Smt. Annapurna Devi, Pandit Pannalal Ghosh, Pandit Nikhil Banerjee, Pandit Timir Baran Bhattacharjee and many others.

In order to understand the contribution of the Seniya Maihar Gharana, interviews of eminent musicians and musicologists of other Gharanas have been taken. Pandit Kumar Prosad Mukherjee (vocalist and musicologist), Shrimati Meera Bandhyopadhyay (vocalist), Surashree Kalyani Roy (Sitar player), Pandit Buddhadev Dasgupta (Sarod player) and Pandit Anindo Chatterjee (Tabla player) expressed their opinions about the contribution of this Gharana. The interviews are recorded hereunder.

6.1 Interview of Pandit Kumar Prosad Mukherjee

QUESTIONNAIRE NO. B1

1. NAME: Pandit Kumar Prosad Mukherjee
2. DATE OF BIRTH: 25th February 1927
3. PLACE OF BIRTH: Allahabad [Uttar Pradesh]
4. SEX: MALE {✓} FEMALE { }
5. GENRE:
   (a) Vocalist { ✓}
   (b) Instrumentalist { }
   (c) Percussionist { }
   (d) Any other: Musicologist
6. MUSICAL TRAINING :

GURUS	YEARS OF TRAINING	GHARANA
1. Dr. Rabindra Lal Roy	Since 1935	na
2. Padmabhushan Mustak Hussain Khan	since 1943	Rampur
3. Ustad Ata Hussain Khan	for 14 years	Agra
4. Ustad Latafat Khan	na	na

7. OPINION REGARDING THE CONTRIBUTION OF THE SENIYA MAIHAR GHARANA TOWARDS THE DEVELOPMENT OF INDIAN CLASSICAL MUSIC

Earlier the *Baj* of Sarod was very uncomplicated – *Gat, Toda, Jhala.* Ustad Allauddin Khan Sahib first introduced the Aalap. Before him no one had done it. Ustad Allauddin Khan Sahab used to plat the complete *Bistar* of any composition he performed.

Annapurna Devi follows his *baj* strictly. Ustad Ali Akbar Khan and Pandit Ravi Shankar are pathfinders just like Baba Allauddin Khan Sahib. For example, Pandit Ravi Shankar has borrowed extensively from Karnatic Music, mainly for the *Taal* portion. Ustad Ali Akbar Khan plays instinctively. He mathematically calculates nothing before a performance. The level to which Ustad Ali Akbar Khan and Pandit Ravi Shankar have raised their style of performance had not even been conceived during Baba Allauddin Khan's time.

Late Nikhil Banerjee was a compendium of all that he had preceded; he was not a pathfinder like Ustad Ali Akbar Khan and Pandit Ravi Shankar. Aashish Khan had learnt from Baba Allauddin Khan Sahib and is an excellent performer.

6.2 Interview of Shrimati Meera Bandhyopadhyay

QUESTIONNAIRE NO. B2

1. NAME: SMT. MEERA BANDHYOPADHYAY
2. DATE OF BIRTH: 1930
3. PLACE OF BIRTH: Meerut
4. SEX: MALE { } FEMALE {✓}
5. GENRE:
   (a) Vocalist {✓}
   (b) Instrumentalist { }
   (c) Percussionist { }
   (d) Any other:
6. MUSICAL TRAINING :

GURUS	YEARS OF TRAINING	GHARANA
1. Sri Sailendra Kumar Chatterjee [father]	till his death	Mixed gharana
2. Pandit D.T Joshi	na	na
3. Sri Chinmoy Lahiri	1948 - 1949	mixed gharana
4. Ustad Bade Ghulam Ali Khan	1950 - 1968	Patiala

7. OPINIONS REGARDING THE CONTRIBUTION OF THE SENIYA MAIHAR GHARANA TOWARDS THE DEVELOPMENT OF INDIAN CLASSICAL MUSIC

Regarding the contribution of the Seniya Maihar Gharana, I would say that the musicians, whom Baba Allauddin Khan Sahib had blessed with his *talim* were transformed into great artistes, for instance Ustad Ali Akbar Khan Sahib, Annapurna Devi, Pandit Ravi Shankar, Shri Timirbaran Bhattacharjee, Shri Pannalal Ghosh, etc. I have interacted with the above musicians and have found that their thinking process is beyond one's imagination. From this we can understand the greatness of Baba Allauddin Khan Sahib.

I have heard Ustad Ali Akbar Khan Sahib's deep and melodious and articulate rendition of *Raag Kanara*. His movements of *Raag Bhairavi*, and the combination of notes are beyond one's imagination. He has also trained some unique disciples, one of them being Pandit Nikhil Banerjee who unfortunately expired quite early.

Pandit Ravi Shankar is a true 'Bharat ratna'. When in 1954, I visited Russia with a cultural delegation, he was with us and I have witnessed some great moments that proved his quality as a true musician.

Annapurna Devi is a versatile genius. I had the opportunity to hear her performance with Pandit Ravi Shankar in a concert in Delhi. Their recital had left me mesmerized.

I have also heard the Sitar recital of Sri Indranil Bhattacharjee. The memory of his melodious presentation still lingers on though he is no more with us.

7. OPINIONS REGARDING THE CONTRIBUTION OF THE SENIYA MAIHAR GHARANA TOWARDS THE DEVELOPMENT OF INDIAN CLASSICAL MUSIC

Among the musicians of this *Gharana* firstly I would like to mention the name of Baba Allauddin Khan Sahib.

There is no one in this world that does not respect him. I first saw him at Nikhil Bango Sangeet Sanmelan organized by Sri Manmatha Ghosh. What I found the most outstanding about Baba was his creation of music.

I have heard Ali Akbar Khan Sahib first at Indira Cinema. The *Raag* he had played was *Nat-Bhairav*. I still remember a *tehai*, which he had played at that concert. I have never seen him watching the audience while performing, rather he remains immersed in his music. His *peshkars* and *laykari* are very appealing and the tonal quality of his instrument is melodious beyond description. His contribution is enormous and he is Music himself... it would be sheer audacity to try and judge his contribution.

I did not have the good fortune of listening to the performance of Smt. Annapurna Devi. However, I do respect the traditional way in which she has been spreading the music of Baba.

Rabi da [Pandit Ravi Shankar] has contributed a lot towards popularizing the Sitar among the masses and its development. He has created so many *talas, layas, raags, raaginis* etc. His students are also a part of his contribution.

I have also heard Aashish Khan's performance. It is very appealing. Lastly I feel an artiste is to be viewed in totality and not only through music.

6.3 Interview of Surashree Kalyani Roy

QUESTIONNAIRE NO. B3

1. NAME: SURASHREE KALYANI ROY
2. DATE OF BIRTH: 29th April, 1931
3. PLACE OF BIRTH: Calcutta
4. SEX: MALE { } FEMALE {✓}
5. GENRE:
   (a) Vocalist { }
   (b) Instrumentalist {✓} Sitar player

(c) Percussionist { }

(d) Any other:

6. MUSICAL TRAINING :

GURUS	YEARS OF TRAINING	GHARANA
1. Sri Nipendra Nath Ganguly	1938/ 1939 onwards	Enayat Khani
2. Ustad Vilayat Hussain Khan	1946/1947 onwards	Imdad Khani

6.4 Interview of Pandit Buddhadev Dasgupta

QUESTIONNAIRE NO. B4

1. NAME: Pandit Buddhadev Dasgupta
2. DATE OF BIRTH: 1st February, 1933
3. PLACE OF BIRTH: Bhagalpur [Bihar]
4. SEX: MALE {✓ } FEMALE { }
5. GENRE:
   (a) Vocalist { }
   (b) Instrumentalist { ✓} Sarod Player
   (c) Percussionist { }
   (d) Any other:
6. MUSICAL TRAINING:

GURUS	YEARS OF TRAINING	GHARANA
1. Pandit Radhia	1942-1981 (39 years)	Shahjahanpur

7. OPINIONS REGARDING

   (A) THE CONTRIBUTION OF THE SENIYA MAIHAR GHARANA TOWARDS THE

DEVELOPMENT OF INDIAN CLASSICAL MUSIC

In Sarod Baba Allauddin Khan Sahib used the *been anga* style of playing. He was the maestro who enlarged the style of *Aalap* in the Sarod. Before this *Aalap* was shorter and the rendition was different.

To me there is no greater performing musician than to Ustad Ali Akbar Khan Sahib. I do not feel there will be any second performing artiste like him. His music has an appealing sensation and listeners get mesmerized. The greatest thing in his music is his unpredictable musiciality. Pandit Ravi Shankar too is a great sitar maestro.

(B) THE CONTRIBUTION OF THE SENIYA MAIHAR GHARANA TOWARDS THE DEVELOPMENT OF THE SAROD

Baba Allauddin Khan changed the fingering in playing the Sarod. He changed the shape, size of the drum and added the four *Thaat* strings in it. Earlier the drum of the Sarod was oval shaped or in other words egg shaped. Baba changed the shape of the drum and made it round. The tonal quality of the instrument was thus improved. In fact, I myself asked Shri Hemen Sen to make my drum round in shape as is common in the Maihar School.

6.5 Interview of Pandit Anindo Chatterjee

QUESTIONNAIRE NO. B5

1. NAME: PANDIT ANINDO CHATTERJEE
2. DATE OF BIRTH: 30th May 1954
3. PLACE OF BIRTH: Duttapukur , North 24 Pargs. Barasat P.S.

4. SEX: MALE { ✓ } FEMALE { }
5. GENRE:
   (a) Vocalist { }
   (b) Instrumentalist { }
   (c) Percussionist { ✓ } Tabla Player
   (d) Any other:
6. MUSICAL TRAINING:

GURUS	YEARS OF TRAINING	GHARANA
1. Pandit Jnan Prakash Ghosh	1960-1977	Farukabad Delhi, Punjab
2. Khalifa Ustad Afaque Hussain Khan	1964-1966	Lucknow

7. OPINIONS REGARDING THE CONTRIBUTION OF THE SENIYA MAIHAR GHARANA TOWARDS THE DEVELOPMENT OF INDIAN CLASSICAL MUSIC

I have been associated with all the maestros of Maihar like Ustad Ali Akbar Khan, Pandit Ravi Shankar, Pandit Nikhil Banerjee and also Shri Indranil Bhattacharjee and Ustad Aashish Khan. However, I had spent a lot of time with Pandit Nikhil Banerjee.

Maihar Gharana's uniqueness to me, a tabla player, is the stress on the maintenance of purity i.e. *suddhata* of a Raag, its expression and uniqueness. Secondly, their *Aalap* is musical, *Jod* has different patterns of expressions and different divisions i.e. *Madhya Jod* etc. I have heard Ustad Ali Akbar Khan Sahib play *Jod* in 5 or 6 *angas*. Similarly in the case of *Aalap* he can show 5 or 6 different *angas*. The expansion of individual notes in case of *Aalap* is a rare phenomenon rarely found in musical renditions of other Gharanas.

My first interaction with Pandit Nikhil Banerjee was in 1967 when I was 13 years old. I used to visit his house and

I have performed many concerts with him. His main contribution was the presentation of *Aalap* and *Jod* ...that was the famous part of Nikhil da. It would often captivate the audience.

In the *gat* portion, Pandit Ravi Shankar has added many rhythmic varieties from South India.

I had performed first with Ustad Ali Akbar Khan Sahib in 1987. I would be mesmerized listening to of Khan Sahib's improvisation of a *Raag*.

I have also witnessed Smt. Annapurna Devi giving *talim* (knowledge) to Pandit Nikhil Banerjee. Like in *raag Kausi Kanara* the necessity of the note *Rishav* was discussed in detail. I feel the expression of a *Raag* in Maihar Gharana is unique. In *Jhala* the variations of right hand is like an ocean where *DA* – comes later. I have also performed with Pandit Hariprasad Chaurasia, Smt. Sharan Rani Mathur, Sri Basant Kabra, Sri Tejendra, Narayan Majumdar and several others.

I have heard excellent concerts of Ustad Aashish Khan and I feel he has everything of his grandfather Baba Allauddin Khan Sahib from the finger movements of the left hand to *bol bani* of the right hand. The *suddhata* of the *Raag-Raagini* is maintained and his *taiyari* is excellent. The rigorous practice that he has gone through is evident in his expertise and it is uncommon in young musicians of today.

6.6 Conclusion

The opinions expressed above by the renowned musicians and musicologists corroborate the fact that the Seniya Maihar Gharana has contributed immensely towards the development of the Sarod and the propagation of Indian Classical in India and abroad. Acharya Baba Allauddin Khan Sahib is considered a legendary figure in the Indian Classical Music scenario. They also acknowledged the contribution of several other celebrated musicians of this Gharana such as Ustad Ali Akbar Khan, Pandit Ravi Shankar, Smt. Annapurna Devi, Pandit Nikhil

Banerjee, Pandit Timir Baran Bhattacharjee, Pandit Pannalal Ghosh, Pandit Hariprasad Chaurasia, Ustad Aashish Khan, Pandit Indranil Bhattacharjee, Pandit Tejendra Narayan Majumdar and others.

7

Conclusion

A detailed study reveals that there are different views regarding the origin of the Sarod. Some scholars claim it to have been originated from the Rabab a versatile instrument, which was either plucked or bowed, commonly played in Afghanistan. It is also claimed that Niyamatullah Khan was the inventor of the Sarod. We also find a group of scholars who claim that the Sarod is a modified version of the Kacchapi Veena or Chitra Veena which was common in ancient India and reference to which is found in Kalidasa's work [450 A.D.].

It is also important to note that, there are many similarities in the structure of Sarod and Rabab, i.e. the fretless fingerboard, the skin over the drum and also the shape of the instrument. The size of the instrument including the drum was increased as the musicians found it convenient to hold and play the instrument keeping it on the lap. When we compare the Rabab and Sarod, we find that there are a lot of similarities between the two instruments. The size of the instruments only differs. After a detailed analysis of all these views it is quite apparent that the Sarod is an instrument, which has originated from the Rabab. After a lot of research and numerous evolutionary changes the Sarod has reached at its present form.

Acharya Allauddin Khan Sahib was a legendary figure in the Indian Classical Music scenario. His contribution towards Indian Classical Music especially the development of the Sarod is unparalleled in the history of Indian Music. Baba Allauddin Khan Sahib brought about several changes in the structure of the Sarod.

1. He changed the shape of the drum from oval or egg shaped to round shape to improve the tonal quality.
2. He added 4 *Jawari strings* to be tuned to appropriate notes of a Raga.
3. He increased the number of *Chikari* strings from 1 to 2; both are tuned to higher register tone *Saa.*
4. He added an optional bass *Pancham string* for playing *Alap* in lower register.
5. He increased the number of *taraf* strings to 15. Earlier sarods had 7 or 11 *taraf* strings.
6. He enlarged the size of the drum from 9 inches to 11 inches in diameter.
7. He standardized the thickness of the steel plate for the fingerboard.

The above changes in the structure of the Sarod converted it into a unique instrument. The design of the present Sarod developed by Baba Allauddin Khan Sahib is considered to be a standard instrument. Presently several Sarod players besides musicians of the Seniya Maihar Gharana use this instrument.

In the technique of playing the Sarod besides notations and writings an Audio Visual C.D. featuring Shri Shyamal Nath and Shri Tejendra Narayan Majumdar has been enclosed (Enclosure 2). The C.D. displays detailed demonstrations covering selection of right gauges of strings, preparing knots, fixing of strings on the Sarod, correct posture with the instrument, holding of the plectrum, the correct fingering with some fingerboard exercises as followed in Seniya Maihar Gharana.

It is well known that, Baba Allauddin Khan Sahib's contribution towards the development of Indian Classical Music is enormous. Several stalwarts of this Gharana such as Ustad Ali Akbar Khan, Pandit Ravi Shankar, Smt. Annapurna Devi, Pandit Pannalal Ghosh, Pandit Nikhil Banerjee, and Ustad Aashish Khan have popularized Indian Classical Music all over the world. Several celebrated disciples of this Gharana have set up Indian Music Schools. They conduct workshops, and lecture demonstrations all over the world and train Indian as well as foreign students thus keeping alive the traditional music of the Seniya Maihar Gharana.

Through the interviews taken of the senior musicians of other Gharanas like Pandit Kumar Prosad Mukherjee, Smt Meera Banerjee, Pandit Buddhadev Dasgupta, Surashree Kalyani Roy, and Pandit Anindo Chatterjee it has been found that they have very high regard and respect for Baba Allauddin Khan Sahib. They have also acknowledged the contribution made by him for development and propagation of Indian Classical Music. According to them, Ustad Ali Akbar Khan and Pandit Ravi Shankar are the living legends and musical geniuses of Seniya Maihar Gharana and their contribution in popularizing Sitar and Sarod in India and abroad is unparalleled.

Bibliography

Ahmed, Mukhtar Ustad (1991): 'Sangeet Research Academy Seminar on Sarod', Western Region, Bombay, p. 58.

Arup Silpa Gosthi (1972): '*Souvenir, published on Ali Akbar Khan*'.

Bagchee, Sandeep (1998): *NAD - Understanding Raga Music*, Eeshwar Publications, Mumbai, pp. 261-223.

Bhattacharya, Timirbaran (2004): *Udoy Pather Sahojatri*, Ananda Publishers Pvt. Ltd.

Chakraborty, Indrani Dr (1991): 'Sangeet Research Academy Seminar on Sarod', Western Region, Bombay, pp. 2-16.

Das Sharma, Amal (1993): *Musicians of India Past and Present*, publisher Naya Prokash, pp. 229-233.

Dasgupta, Buddhadev Pt. (1991):'Sangeet Research Academy Seminar on Sarod', Western Region, Bombay, pp. 37-41.

'Desh' (8th Baisakh, 1363).

Dhar Chowdhury, Sisirkona (1982): '*Ustad Alauddin Khan: The Great Maestro*' Journal Dept. of Instrumental Music. Vol. 2, pp. 46-54.

Gangopadhyay, Sree (1991): 'Sangeet Research Academy Seminar on Sarod', Western Region Bombay, pp. 50-57.

Ganguly, Hirendra Kumar (1982): "*Contributions of Alauddin Khan to Hindustani Music*", Journal Dept. of Instrumental Music, Rabindra Bharati University, Kolkata, pp. 12-17.

Ghosh, Anuradha (1990): *Ustad Alauddin Khan - The Legend of Music*, published by Govt. of India, pp. 21-38.

Ghosh, Subhomoy (1st Baisakh 1381): *Amar Katha - Alauddin Khan*, Published by Ananda Publishers Pvt. Ltd., pp. 7-78.

Guha, Uma (1999): *Saint Maestro Baba Alauddin*, publisher Sahityika, pp. 7-16.

Kasliwal, Suneera Dr. (2001): *Classical Musical Instruments*, published by Rupa and Co., pp. 153-161, 166 -175.

Khan, Aashish Ustad (1993): '*The Contribution of Maihar Gharana to the Evolution and Technique of Sarod*' Souvenir Published by Deba Prasad Banerjee.

Khan, Aashish Ustad (1991): 'Sangeet Research Academy Seminar on Sarod', Western Region, Bombay, pp. 17-24.

McNeil, Adrian (1983): *The Emergence of the Sarod in Hindustani Music*, unpublished PhD thesis submitted to Dept. of Music, Monash University.

Menon, Raghava R. (1995): *The Penguin Dictionary of Indian Classical Music*, Penguin Books India Pvt. Ltd., pp. 16-169.

Miner, Allyn (1997): *Sitar and Sarod in the 18th and 19th Centuries*, Performing Art Series, Volume VII, Published by Motilal Banarsidass Publishers Pvt. Ltd., Delhi, pp. 60-69.

Navras Records Ltd. Jugalbandi (Duet) Series, Pandit Jasraj and Pandit Hariprasad Chaurasia, Vol. 1, NRCC 0018.

Roy, Sinha Ajoy (1992): *Musing on Music,* published by Sri Adinath Bhattacharya [Director of Culture] Govt. of West Bengal, pp. 61-66.

Ruckert, George (1991): *The Classical Music of North India,* Volume One, published by East Bay Books, Saint Louis, Missouri, p. 367.

Singh, Thakur Jaidev (1982): *'Contributions of Acharya Alauddin Khan to Hindustani Music',* Journal Dept. of Instrumental Music, Rabindra Bharati University, Kolkata, pp. 4-11.

Singh, Thakur Jaidev (1995): *Indian Music,* published by Sangeet Research Academy, Calcutta, pp. 466-467.

Souvenir published on Baba Allauddin Khan.

Tagore, S.M. (1976): *'Yantra Kosh'.*

Vir, Ram Avatar (1983): *Musical Instruments of India (History and Developments),* Pankaj Publications, New Delhi, pp. 61-62.

Wade, Bonnie. C (1999): *Music in India (The Classical Traditions),* Monohar Publishers, New Delhi, pp. 98-101.

Websites Consulted

http://www.ammp.com/bio.html

http://web.axelero.hu/andkozma/ravi1.jpg

http://www.aacm.org/aacm/teaching.htm

http://web.axelero.hu/andkozma/sishya.htm

http://www.aoe.vt.edu/~boppe/MUSIC/GHAR/sarod.html

http://banglapedia.search.com.bd/HT/K-0169.HTM

http://www.divinesarod.com/sarod.html

http://www.fabmart.com/stores/hindustanifest/hcallauddin.asp

http://www.gwalior.com/Articles view.asp/article-id=10

http://homepage.mac.com/tjorgensen/maihar.html

http://music.calarts.edu/~bansuri/annapurna.html

http://www.pathcom/~ercip/mi_bahadur2.jpg

http://www.pifano.nl/Images/PannalalGhosh.jpg

http://www.ravishankar.com

http://www.ravishankar.org/foundation-frame.html

http://www.rajeevtaranath.com/

http://www.silverbushmusic.com

http://www.silverbushmusic.com/sarodeAAK.jpg

http://www.womeninfoline.com/culture/music/ustadaliakbarkhan.asp

http://www.westbengal.com/aashish/

Personal Communications

Ustad Aashish Khan [2003-04]

Ustad Ali Akbar Khan Sahib [2003]

Smt. Ameena Perera [2003-04]

Sri. Amit Roy [2003]

Smt. Anindita Mukherjee [2003]

Sri. Anindo Banerjee [2003]

Sri. Bhaskar Gupta [2003]

Sri. Birendranath Banerjee [2003]

Sri. Debi Prasad Chatterjee [2003]

Pandit Deepak Chowdhury [2003]

Sri. Dulal Chandra Kanji [2003]

Dr. E.S. Perera [2003]

Sri. Gopeshwar Bandyopadhyay [2003]

Sri. Gour S. Dasgupta [2003]

Sri. Hemen Chandra Sen [2003]

Sri. Manoj Barua [2003]

Smt. Namita Chatterjee [2003]

Sri. Nityanand Haldipur [2003]

Sri Partha Sarathi Choudhury [2003]

Sri. Purbayan Chatterjee [2003]

Dr. Rajeev Chakraborty [2003]

Smt. Sahana Khan [2003]

Sri. Shyamal Nath [2002-04]

Sri. Somesh Chatterjee [2003]

Sri. Somjit Dasgupta [2003]

Sri. Supriyo Banerjee [2003]

Pandit Tejendra Narayan Majumdar [2002-04]

Smt. Uma Guha [2003]

Smt. Usha Majumdar [2003]

Smt. Zubeda Khan [2003-04]

INDEX